# 105
# DAYS
## *of*
# PRAYER

## JACKIE
# MCCULLOUGH

**Destiny Image® Publishers, Inc.**
P.O. Box 310
Shippensburg, PA 17257-0310

*"Speaking to the Purposes of God for This Generation
and for the Generations to Come"*

ISBN 978-0-7394-6264-5

Printed in the U.S.A.

# DEDICATION

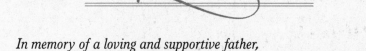

*In memory of a loving and supportive father,*
THE REVEREND PERCIVAL HERRON GRAVAL PHILLIPS

*In honor of a praying and loving mother,*
EVANGELIST KETURAH ELIZABETH HENRY PHILLIPS

Their spiritual and emotional investment has helped to make me who I am today.

# ACKNOWLEDGMENTS

Special Thanks...

...To Rev. Katrina Huffman, Rev. Trish McLeod, and Rev. Amie Gardner for helping to make this book come to pass.

...To Pastor Robyn Edwards, Pastor George Hyman, Jr., and Pastors Cleve and Margaret Taylor, the Executive Pastors of Beth Rapha, for your prayers and support.

...To the pastors, ministers and members of The International Gathering at Beth Rapha. Thank you for your love, kindness, and prayers. I consider myself blessed to be your pastor.

...To Daughters of Rizpah for your administrative support.

...To Pastor Sheila K. Knight, Pastor Jonathan L. McKnight, and Pastor Sandra Tabron for being so supportive and prayerful.

# CONTENTS

# PREFACE

*Transparency* is a word foreign to our present-day prayer vocabulary. So many believers want to be acknowledged as intercessors and prayer warriors, but few want to be intimate and transparent with the Lord. Instead, our prayer lives have been opaque with meaningless rhetoric that does not reflect our true heart.

The first step to transparency is to admit that our hearts are deeply affected by issues and challenges of life, such as imprisonment, abandonment, rejection, fear, anxiety, and boredom. The next steps are to be honest and open with the Lord, and then surrender to His will. A surrendered heart is a transparent heart.

True intimacy in prayer is realized when you come seeking His agenda—not asking Him to approve yours. A transparent heart is a heart that seeks to conform and to pray the will of the Father in spite of how he or she may feel.

How do we deal with the effects of the issues of life and their impact on our spirits? Seek the counsel of God and meditate on His Word: "Blessed is the man that walketh not in the counsel of the ungodly, nor standeth in the way of sinners, nor sitteth in the seat of the scornful. But his delight is in the law of the Lord; and in His law doth he meditate day and night" (Ps. 1:1-2). Meditation requires that you engage in thought concerning the Scripture. It suggests that your contemplation will activate godly instruction in your life.

Meditating on the Scriptures and obeying what they say will render transparency in prayer, in praise, and in worship. When you move the issues of life from your heart to the Lord's hands, you can expect to be a "tree planted by the rivers of water, that bringeth forth his fruit in his season" (Ps. 1:3a). When you are honest with the Lord, you can expect Him to move greatly in your life.

This book is intended to help you ground your prayer life in the eternal reality that will help you to expose your heart to the One who tries the reins of your heart. It is intended to show you the struggles of life and how you can take them all to God in prayer with confidence that He will bend His ear to your mouth and answer according to His Word.

Expect answers as you put your *all on the altar.*

*—J.E.M.*

# FOREWORD

Traditional views of prayer have often caused us to articulate prayers that are irrelevant and ineffective. Because of an inability or unwillingness to take ownership of our faults and true feelings, we tend to pray amiss, uttering words that are ritualistic and unrelated to our realities.

False perceptions, inner conflicts, and self-delusion can cause us to offer prayers that do not really speak to our needs or address our inner and outer struggles. A person may spend time praying for God to help him love his enemies, when the real issue that needs to be addressed is his combative personality that evokes feelings of enmity from others. Another prays for healing, when the real need is a change of attitude so that the healing can take place. In short, prayer is at its best when it not only leads us into the presence of the Almighty, but when it also brings the pray-er to a place of self-discovery and soul-searching. The primary way for believers to grow spiritually and emotionally is to allow prayer time to be a time of confession and honest self-assessment.

The prayers offered in this book by Pastor Jacqueline McCullough illuminate the reality that the only prayers that achieve true intimacy with God are the ones that are prayed in complete honesty. She reminds us that holding back or misrepresentation in our conversations with God can only prevent our spiritual advancement and healing. I believe that this most poignant and life-altering book shows us how to truly pray with God-confidence and find a closer relationship with the God whose most fervent desire is for us to draw closer and rest in His love.

As you read this book, let it release you to new levels of transparency with God. Let her prayers motivate you to pray your own prayers with candor and commitment to the Word and the way of the divine.

Rev. Dr. M. Elaine McCollins Flake
Copastor, The Greater Allen Cathedral
Jamaica, New York

# Prayer and Purpose

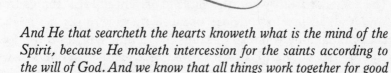

*And He that searcheth the hearts knoweth what is the mind of the Spirit, because He maketh intercession for the saints according to the will of God. And we know that all things work together for good to them that love God, to them who are the called according to His purpose* (Romans 8:27-28).

What is the purpose of prayer? How does it work out God's purpose in our lives? If you have purpose, you have a sense of direction. But, finding our purpose is often not the central issue. The heart of the matter is yielding to God in prayer physically, intellectually, spiritually, and emotionally.

Prayer, when done correctly, encompasses the entire person. So the purpose of prayer is to get all of you involved. You cannot pray effectively with your mouth separated from your spirit. Jesus spoke of the Pharisees in this respect: "He answered and said unto them, Well hath Esaias prophesied of you hypocrites, as it is written, This people honoureth Me with their lips, but their heart is far from Me" (Mk. 7:6). So it's possible to engage in the ritual of prayer without the devotion of prayer. But if you really want to be engaged in God's purpose, all of you must be involved in prayer. For effective prayer involves the whole being—the spirit, the soul, and the body. It takes the whole person to pray, and prayer affects the entire person as a result.

Something wonderful and supernatural happens to you in intercession when you're submitted to God in your heart and lifestyle. As you pray, God's purposes are accomplished in your life, because there is a plan being worked in you. By engaging in earnest prayer to Him, a transformation occurs within you to bring you to the will and purpose of God in your life.

Those who give all in prayer receive much or all in the answer. Whatever you put in is what you get out. Many times we pray for things, while at the same time, parts of our lives have not been submitted to God. If He asks us to do something that is not in keeping with our desire, we often won't do it—but that's where the answer is. If you pray for a relationship to be healed, and the Lord requires you to apologize, what happens if you refuse? You simply forfeit your answer. A prevalent practice in the Church today is that we compartmentalize ourselves when we come to God. We give Him only what is convenient. But we must give Him everything.

The saints of history and the Bible experienced great things from God, and walked in His purpose because they were given to much prayer. Any biography you read of saints like Smith Wigglesworth, John Knox, John Calvin, Martin Luther, or Aimee Semple McPherson will demonstrate to you that these people had a prayer life. Bishop C.H. Mason, the founder of the Church Of God In Christ denomination, said that his greatest testimony was that he prayed all day. You can't expect to have a flimsy, halfhearted prayer life and simultaneously do great things for God. It simply doesn't work that way. The greater the prayer life, the stronger the anointing. The greater the prayer life, the greater the experience—and the greater the purpose.

God must have wholehearted men and women through whom He can work out His purposes and plans. But He cannot use people who are halfhearted, inconsistent, or unstable. That's why the Bible says in James 1:7 that an unstable person will not get anything from God. Instability is one of the gravest problems in our churches. Wholehearted commitment that manifests the purpose of God comes only as we yield to His purpose in prayer.

Purpose involves our ambitions, goals, and aspirations. But God's purposes are so different from what we are trained to desire or expect. In church, we often have major dreams, visions, and illusions of grandeur. The issue is that some of these dreams and visions have nothing to do with the purpose of God in most of our lives.

Many of us look at other people and see how they have come to a certain point. As a result, we think that's where we are going. But do you know where these people have gone? If you knew the real story and considered the price, sacrifice, and heartache they had to endure to get there, you wouldn't dare think of traveling the same road. Please do not sit and envy someone's position and power with illusions of greatness.

Pray into your own purpose until your mind, will, intellect, and spirit become conformed to the will of God. It is then that the purpose of God for you will unfold.

Praying in purpose is about coming to God without an agenda. Even if I do have an agenda, I am willing to lay my agenda before the Lord, if necessary. I must be ready, willing, and able to forget my agenda, if it is not in keeping with His will. There is nothing wrong with coming to God with an agenda, but always leave it "open." You can't serve or please God with an adamant, strong-willed attitude.

Even as you read this book, your purposes are being examined and scrutinized by the Lord. As you think about all the things you hope to be and become, ask yourself, *Are they in keeping with God's will?* If God has designated you to be a vessel of honor, that is what you will become. But if He has designated you to be a vessel of clay, can you accept that? Many people die angry and frustrated, because they have never said, "Thy will be done."

I challenge you to surrender yourself wholly to the Lord, that you may fulfill His purposes for your life, and experience the fullness of His joy.

—J.E.M.

# PRAYER OF AWAKENING

Father, I am suddenly aware of a weakness that has hindered me for years and has kept me from embracing my purpose in life. God, I hear Your Word. I believe Your Word. But I do not confess Your Word. Society has taught me to avoid accountability, so I have learned the fine art of indifference.

Yes, Lord, that is why I am not completely delivered! Yes, Lord, that is why I am not empowered and free!

Today, I forsake indifference and arise to own this Word, possess this Word, and release this Word through my mouth in the name of Jesus. I am determined to come in line with Your will for my life.

Lord, I know that as I agree with Your Word and Your will for my life, I am connecting with my divine purpose and forsaking a life of misery. Thank You for the peace, joy, happiness, and fulfillment that come with connecting with Your purpose. Thank You for a new heart and a committed will to travel my directed path in life. Amen.

*Therefore He says:"Awake, you who sleep, arise from the dead, and Christ will give you light"* ( Ephesians 5:14 NKJV).

*Death and life are in the power of the tongue, and those who love it will eat its fruit* (Proverbs 18:21 NKJV).

*...for every purpose of the Lord shall be performed...* (Jeremiah 51:29).

# PRAYER OF LOVE

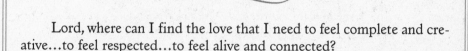

Lord, where can I find the love that I need to feel complete and creative...to feel respected...to feel alive and connected?

Is my desire to give and receive this kind of love in this present world just a fantasy? Certainly this world focuses on physical appearance and constantly instructs me in the carnal lessons of love with little attention to inward character.

But I am ready to empty myself of all that I've been taught and all that I have seen and experienced as it relates to my understanding of love. I will maintain this emotional catharsis in order to be whole in my soul.

Ah, Lord, make me ready to walk in a new spiritual journey of love. Father, I am willing to undergo surgery in order to untangle the web of a loveless life. Cut away, I pray, the dark memories of abuse and abandonment. Cut away, I pray, the pain that fills the crevices of my mind and the resentment that clutters the arteries of my heart. I want to be whole, Lord. Heal me and I'll be healed!

Guide me so that I won't make the same mistakes! Forgive me, merciful Father, for entangling myself in relationships that You did not ordain! And help me to forgive myself so that I can freely embrace the next level of charity...apart from my past. Take it away, Lord, so that I can be free to see life and love in its true form.

Lord, speak to me in ways that I have never heard before. Unveil Yourself in ways I have never witnessed. Thank You, Lord, for the freshness of Your presence and the graciousness of Your mercy in this area of my need. Thank You for teaching me to love without inhibitions. Amen.

[Love] *bears all things, believes all things,*
*hopes all things, endures all things*
(1 Corinthians 13:7 NKJV)

*Heal me, O Lord, and I shall be healed...*
(Jeremiah 17:14).

*I love the Lord, because He has heard*
*my voice and my supplications*
(Psalm 116:1 NKJV).

# PRAYER FOR TIME

Forgive me for ignoring Your wooing and for procrastinating in making the decision to do what You have commanded. Lord, please lessen the consequences of delayed obedience, which is disobedience. Grant me grace, I pray, for the wasted time, wasted resources, and wasted efforts.

This is teaching me to sense godly timing. The spirit of slothfulness, the spirit of haste, and the spirit of indifference have made me unconscious of Your skillful maneuvers in all of my circumstances. Help me to redeem the time.

Thank You for Your patience, God. Only You understand how I approach my journey in life. I am waking up from my slumber. I am alive and alert. I am conscious and sensitive. I am ready to move when You say, "Move."

Thank You for this moment in prayer, Lord. I decree that my time will be in sync with Your purpose and will for my life. Glory be to the wise and majestic Author and Finisher of all things. Amen.

*Slothfulness casteth into a deep sleep...*
(Proverbs 19:15).

*Awake to righteousness, and sin not; for some have not the
knowledge of God: I speak this to your shame*
(1 Corinthians 15:34).

*Wherefore he saith, Awake thou that sleepest, and arise
from the dead, and Christ shall give thee light. See then
that ye walk circumspectly, not as fools, but as wise,
redeeming the time, because the days are evil*
(Ephesians 5:14-16).

# PRAYER FOR MEMORIES

I looked through my picture albums and walked into a time capsule. Still images of friends and loved ones came alive before my eyes. Feelings, failures, touches, words, plans, hopes, and dreams were relived in flashes, in pieces, in volumes, and in visions.

Lord, I sense Your presence, and I know that You are allowing closure to unresolved issues—issues I have denied for years. They're so painful, Lord, that they cause my tear glands to swell with heaviness.

It's a weary and laborious process, but I welcome the change in my spirit. Lord, create a new me. Restore my mind, empower my spirit, and refill my soul with the light of Your Word. Reveal the truth I have avoided for so long.

Thank You, Lord, for the courage to confront the memories without succumbing to the tyranny of pain. Thank You for guiding me, though I resist at times, to the place where the present neutralizes the past and the power of Your eternal purpose washes over the memories. In Jesus' name I pray, Amen.

*Create in me a clean heart, O God;*
*and renew a right spirit within me*
(Psalm 51:10).

*I will lift up mine eyes unto the hills, from whence*
*cometh my help. My help cometh from the Lord,*
*which made heaven and earth*
(Psalm 121:1-2).

*Thus hath the Lord dealt with me in the days wherein He*
*looked on me, to take away my reproach among men*
(Luke 1:25).

# PRAYER FOR DELIVERANCE FROM BITTERNESS

We came out of the same womb, drank from the same breast, sat on the same lap, yet saw the same world differently. For years I sought to change her, compete with her, and loved to hate her.

We refrained from talking. We grew apart. I refused to forgive. But in praise and worship, You showed me how ugly bitterness made me.

Lord, You are helping me to see my sister as You see her. I thank You, because through prayer, You are helping me to accept my sister's differences, celebrate her victories, recognize her purpose, and work with her downfalls.

Learning to love my sister in this way is liberating. Lord, grant me insight and continue to teach me to be a true friend to a sister I almost lost. God, You are so precious to me. Amen.

*Behold, for peace I had great bitterness: but Thou hast in love to my soul delivered it from the pit of corruption: for Thou hast cast all my sins behind Thy back*
(Isaiah 38:17).

*Let all bitterness, and wrath, and anger, and clamour, and evil speaking, be put away from you, with all malice: and be ye kind one to another, tenderhearted, forgiving one another, even as God for Christ's sake hath forgiven you*
(Ephesians 4:31-32).

*Beloved, let us love one another: for love is of God; and every one that loveth is born of God, and knoweth God. He that loveth not knoweth not God; for God is love*
(1 John 4:7-8).

# PRAYER FROM THE SICKBED

All the visitors are gone and my loved one is asleep in the chair. In the midst of my sedation, in the cloudiness of my conscious state, I can hear You, feel You, and sense You. A number of thoughts are running through my head. Doubts about healing erode my faith. The fear of leaving my offspring chills my spine, but praising You with my lips makes the darkness light.

This prayer is only a whisper, but is as bitter as Hannah's for her Samuel. I wait as Daniel waited—weary with fasting, seeking an answer, looking for the strength of Your Word. Looking for a change and not seeing it has made me as cynical as Sarah who laughed about having Isaac.

But I am going to pull strength from the weary fibers of my flesh and cry to You one more night. In this prayer, I will not languish and I will not beg. I will trust Your grace, I will embrace Your mercy, and I will rest in Your balm. Let Your virtue flow through me, in a way that the doctors will know that You are able to heal supernaturally and completely. Hear my prayer, O Lord. Amen.

*For the grave cannot praise Thee, death can not celebrate
Thee: they that go down into the pit cannot hope for Thy
truth. The living, the living, he shall praise Thee, as I do this
day: the father to the children shall make known Thy truth*
(Isaiah 38:18-19).

*The sorrows of death compassed me....In my distress
I called upon the Lord, and cried unto my God:
He heard my voice out of His temple, and my cry
came before Him, even into His ears*
(Psalm 18:4a,6).

*...If thou wilt diligently hearken to the voice of the Lord
thy God, and wilt do that which is right in His sight,
and wilt give ear to His commandments, and keep
all His statutes, I will put none of these diseases
upon thee...for I am the Lord that healeth thee*
(Exodus 15:26).

*And Jesus saith unto him, I will come and heal him*
(Matthew 8:7).

# PRAYER OF GUIDANCE

I was always afraid of being one of them. You know what "one of them" means: those people who seem as though they can't make a move without You. They are always talking about what You said, what You did, and who You are.

I believed for so long that You made *me* intelligent, independent, creative, resourceful, and charismatic. All I had to do was use these gifts to chart my course and determine *my own* destiny. But now I am older, weaker, and wiser—wiser, because my illusions have been blown away by the wind and my dreams have escaped my grasp like vapor.

I need You "every hour," as my mother used to say. I must trust You for everything, just like Proverbs 3:5 and 6 say, and walk with a prayer presence. My spirit says, "Yes, Lord!"

*In whom also we have obtained an inheritance, being predes-
tinated according to the purpose of Him who worketh
all things after the counsel of His own will: that we should
be to the praise of His glory, who first trusted in Christ*
(Ephesians 1:11-12).

*Trust in the Lord with all thine heart; and lean not
unto thine own understanding. In all thy ways
acknowledge Him, and He shall direct thy paths*
(Proverbs 3:5-6).

*Howbeit when He, the Spirit of truth, is come, He will
guide you into all truth: for He shall not speak of
Himself; but whatsoever He shall hear, that shall He
speak: and He will show you things to come*
(John 16:13).

# PRAYER OF GRATITUDE

My heart speaks forcefully, pounding with expressions of gratefulness. Through my lips, I pour out thanksgiving. Yes, I am conscious of all my blessings, Lord. I count them all—great and small.

After all these years, I am coming to understand that "all things work together for the good...." I love You so much, Lord, and I am confident that good is coming out of every bad situation.

I thank You for the days that I misunderstood Your moves. I realize now that each move has brought me to a place that I would not have received for myself. Thank You for taking me down paths I did not want to travel. I never dreamed that Your move would be so much bigger, wiser, purer, and richer.

I thank You for the safe rides even on the bumpy roads. I thank You for the hugs and the shrugs from the same people. Thank You for the slow return of the blessings and seemingly quick responses to prayer.

I thank You for the valleys, plateaus, and mountains of experience...and the calm, windless movement of time. Yes, "in everything," today, and hopefully tomorrow, I give thanks, Lord!

*How precious also are Thy thoughts unto me,*
*O God! how great is the sum of them! If I should*
*count them, they are more in number than the*
*sand: when I awake, I am still with Thee*
(Psalm 139:17-18).

*And he that searcheth the hearts knoweth what is the*
*mind of the Spirit, because He maketh intercession for the*
*saints according to the will of God. And we know that all*
*things work together for good to them that love God, to*
*them who are the called according to His purpose*
(Romans 8:27-28).

*A gracious woman retaineth honor...*
(Proverbs 11:16).

# PRAYER FOR BAD RELATIONSHIPS

Lord, deliver me out of this empty and meaningless relationship. It's absolutely ridiculous! The type of people I entangle myself with is unbelievable.

I know that I have a propensity to attach myself to people and circumstances that are contradictory to the inner process You've started in me for Your glory. But today, I want You to dwell in me so richly that I will attract godliness and beauty in my life. I'm tired of bad, fruitless, draining relationships. They are fatal!

Lord, please cover my neediness until I become filled with Your purpose. Do not leave any place unguarded until I sense the strength of Your presence. I am coming out, Lord, in Your name, to go into the paradise of true friendship with You and my covenant friends for life. You are my way out, my Jesus. I bless Your name.

*Trust in Him at all times; ye people, pour out*
*your heart before Him: God is a refuge for us*
(Psalm 62:8).

*Henceforth I call you not servants...*
*but I have called you friends*
(John 15:15).

*He shall cover thee with His feathers, and under His*
*wings shalt thou trust: His truth shall be thy shield*
*and buckler....Because thou hast made the Lord, which*
*is my refuge, even the most High, thy habitation*
(Psalm 91:4,9).

# PRAYER TO COVER A GOOD MARRIAGE

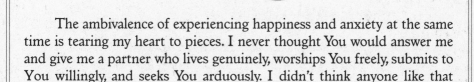

The ambivalence of experiencing happiness and anxiety at the same time is tearing my heart to pieces. I never thought You would answer me and give me a partner who lives genuinely, worships You freely, submits to You willingly, and seeks You arduously. I didn't think anyone like that existed...but You saw fit to bring this person into my life.

It is the relationship with You, Lord, which draws me into the freedom to trust, to confess, to reach out, and to love this person in return. I stand in awe, knowing that two spirits can become one in a way where there is no shame, guilt, dishonor, disrespect, or defamation. We are free to love You and express our love to each other. What a blessing!

Thank You, Lord, for teaching my partner how to love me and for showing me how to love my partner. Cover us, Lord, and continue to teach us how to stay under the shadow of Your wings. Should we ever stray from Your covering, maneuver us back to that secret place.

I close this prayer with a calm assurance of Your divine love and protection, knowing that Your desires will be fulfilled in our lives. Amen, and thank God!

*And they were both naked, the man*
*and his wife, and were not ashamed*
(Genesis 2:25).

*He that dwelleth in the secret place of the most*
*High shall abide under the shadow of the Almighty*
(Psalm 91:1).

*Husbands, love your wives, even as Christ*
*also loved the church, and gave Himself for it*
(Ephesians 5:25).

# PRAYER FOR THE WOMB OF THE PREGNANT MOTHER

The baby is moving, turning, and floating within the belly of my being. I am utterly amazed at the transformation of my body and the development of my child. My life has changed, especially my appetite. I can't sleep comfortably in bed anymore. I can't even tie my shoelaces. It's all new. It's all different, but it's all life.

Tell me, Lord, how did You create such a marvelous, miraculous, spectacular design? It is so far beyond my human comprehension.

I ask that You insulate this baby all the way to the delivery room. Grant me kind medical personnel to facilitate this birth. I pray for a natural birth, but if assisted birth is necessary, then guide it with Your powerful hand. Give my husband the stamina to work with me during the delivery. Make the moment unforgettable for the both of us.

Let our newborn cry with the sound of life and freedom. Let the baby's fingers and toes curl with strength to grip the world. Let us hold, feed, and caress our little one into the nurturing love that You gave us.

Thank You for a strong, healthy, and complete birthing experience. Thank You for changing our lives forever.

*...Who are those with thee? And he said, The children which God hath graciously given thy servant*
(Genesis 33:5).

*Shall I bring to the birth, and not cause to bring forth? saith the Lord: shall I cause to bring forth, and shut the womb? saith thy God*
(Isaiah 66:9).

*...it pleased God, who separated me from my mother's womb, and called me by His grace*
(Galatians 1:15).

# PRAYER FOR SUCCESS

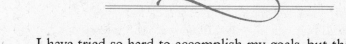

I have tried so hard to accomplish my goals, but they tend to lead me down a dead-end street. Father, please help me find the way to make my dreams come true. I do not want to make any more plans or attempt to carry out any former plans, until I hear from You. Are my goals in line with Your goals for me?

Maybe I'm a little too driven to accomplish certain things by a certain time in order to prove my self-worth. I try to make meaningful decisions about my ministry, but it seems to go nowhere. I try to make decisions in my career, and again, they go nowhere. I try to make decisions about my personal life (or lack thereof), but they go no further than a thought. What is all of this about?

Lord, help me to focus on Your plan for my life and not to expend energy on my plans, because they are going nowhere. I want Your plan, Your will, and Your purpose for my life.

How did I ever miss this truth? Teach me to hear You clearly; teach me to follow You closely. Teach me, O Lord, to trust You fully. I will get a journal, Lord, and sit with my Bible open so that I can chart this course with Your Word and through the Holy Spirit. Lift the spirit of anxiety from me and let me learn the power of waiting on "unanswered prayers."

Thank You, Lord, for the peace, because I'm laying down my agenda with a mind to follow Your agenda. I thank You that Your name is a strong tower that I can run into and find refuge. I sense Your presence, and I know that my journey will be different as I set my affections on things above. Thank You for establishing me, settling me, and placing me where You predestined me to be. Amen.

*This book of the law shall not depart out of thy mouth;*
*but thou shalt meditate therein day and night, that*
*thou mayest observe to do according to all that is*
*written therein: for then thou shalt make thy way*
*prosperous, and then thou shalt have good success*
(Joshua 1:8).

*For I know the thoughts and plans that I have for you,*
*says the Lord, thoughts and plans for welfare and peace*
*and not for evil, to give you hope in your final outcome*
(Jeremiah 29:11 AMP).

*But seek (aim at and strive after) first of all His kingdom*
*and His righteousness (His way of doing and being right),*
*and then all these things taken together will be given you*
*besides. So do not worry or be anxious about tomorrow,*
*for tomorrow will have worries and anxieties of its own*
(Matthew 6:33-34a AMP).

# PRAYER FOR INSIGHT

Lord, it amazes me that things that are not visible strongly influence my life. My pragmatic side pulls me to reason to find the perfect logical explanation; but, I hear a higher call.

I feel You tugging at my will, my intellect, and my spirit. This is a time when I must not fear what I cannot explain or what seems impossible or ridiculous. Your Word has become dearer to my soul. The more I struggle to live my life, the more I am gravely impacted by the spiritual realm. But I thank You for more clarity when I read the Bible.

I want to walk in the path of righteousness and freedom. This is my earnest prayer: *Illuminate me with Your presence so that I can have Your light and Your life, Your power and Your peace.* Lord, I lift my hands to receive all that You have for me. I open my ears to hear what Your Spirit will say. I lift my eyes to see the path You have determined for me to walk in at this time.

Light, come! Vision, unfold! Understanding, come forth in the name of Jesus!

*Who hath ears to hear, let him hear*
(Matthew 13:9).

*So that thou incline thine ear unto wisdom,*
*and apply thine heart to understanding*
(Proverbs 2:2).

*The entrance of Thy words giveth light;*
*it giveth understanding unto the simple*
(Psalm 119:130).

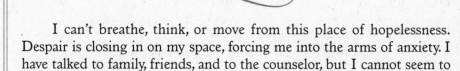
# PRAYER FROM
# A TIGHT PLACE

I can't breathe, think, or move from this place of hopelessness. Despair is closing in on my space, forcing me into the arms of anxiety. I have talked to family, friends, and to the counselor, but I cannot seem to break out of my closed quarters. Lord, it feels as though my life is spinning out of control.

Life has squeezed me before, but not in such a tight grip as this. I am overwhelmed with my problems that seem to be without solutions. It has been one thing after another, Lord. I am so depressed. I can't be around others without engaging in some quarrel. All of my thoughts are negative. This is not the way You designed for me to live day by day.

If I have to stay in this place, then help me to breathe Your breath, think Your thoughts, and live Your life. This is the only way that I can make it through and come into my enlarged place. If I could only see some sign of change, I would feel a little more confident. Father, help me! I know there is no failure in You and no shadow of turning in Your Word.

Thank You for regulating my breathing as I pray. Thank You for helping me to stretch a little in this tight place. Thank You for the circumstances in life that force me to release myself in prayer. Though the places in my life may become tight, I will press my way in prayer, speak and believe Your Word in prayer, and wait on Your promises in prayer. Even in this rigid place, Lord, I thank You, because You are fashioning me according to the counsel of Your will.

*O Lord, Thou hast searched me, and known me*
*(Psalm 139:1).*

*Thou hast turned for me my mourning into dancing:*
*Thou hast put off my sackcloth, and girded me with gladness*
*(Psalm 30:11).*

*As His divine power has given to us all things that*
*pertain to life and godliness, through the knowledge*
*of Him who called us by glory and virtue*
*(2 Peter 1:3 NKJV).*

# PRAYER FOR LAUGHTER

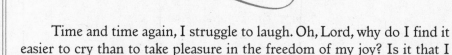

Time and time again, I struggle to laugh. Oh, Lord, why do I find it easier to cry than to take pleasure in the freedom of my joy? Is it that I am so used to suffering that I have forgotten how to enjoy the moment?

I ask You, dear Lord, to reveal the damage that chokes my joy. Help me to acknowledge it, deal with it, and release it. Help me to regain the ability to move readily into hilarity. I know that laughter is good medicine. I know that when I laugh, it lifts the gloom and despair from my spirit. I know You desire for me to have a merry heart. I release the hesitancy and take pleasure in my jolly moments.

My sincere desire is to live this life on a different plane. Pain surpasses the laughter roaring in my belly; my pleasure is suppressed by sorrow. Move the laughter upward and I will bellow without restraint. By faith, I receive my time of celebration in laughter without fear. Thank You, Lord!

*He will yet fill your mouth with*
*laughter and your lips with shouts of joy*
(Job 8:21 NIV).

*A feast is made for laughter...*
(Ecclesiastes 10:19).

*...God hath made me to laugh, so that*
*all that hear will laugh with me*
(Genesis 21:6).

# Prayer in Times of Embarrassment

Well, Lord, I feel quite unnerved and stripped of my pride. This experience has left me quite humbled, even ashamed. I tried so hard to correct my mistakes before they became public, but it was too late. Now I have to face myself while others are looking.

I can imagine how David felt when he numbered the people and prepared himself to endure Your punishment. He chose to fall on Your mercy, God, rather than to trust the mercy of people. Please help me to clean these areas of my life and to learn my lessons so that I will never visit this place again.

I have often looked at others in their embarrassment and wondered how they got there. I also remarked on why they would not leave that place. But now that I am wallowing in my mud, I understand that it is not always a quick turnaround that is experienced, but sometimes a slow walking out.

Lord, help me to walk out of this darkness and into Your light. I can't do it by myself because I am cloaked in sinful flesh, but I pray for Your Holy Spirit to quicken me to move courageously, carefully, and willingly out of this degrading position.

Thank You, Lord! I am committed to developing a new mind. I will be conscious of these failures, focusing on the lessons learned and applying the wisdom gained. Thank You for covering my shame and for not casting me out of Your presence.

*But now thus saith the Lord that created thee, O Jacob, and He that formed thee, O Israel, Fear not: for I have redeemed thee, I have called thee by thy name; thou art Mine*
(Isaiah 43:1).

*And be renewed in the spirit of your mind*
(Ephesians 4:23).

*He shall cover thee with His feathers, and under His wings shalt thou trust: His truth shall be thy shield and buckler*
(Psalm 91:4).

# PRAYER FOR THE DEDICATION OF A MUSICAL HEART

Lord, I woke up this morning with a wonderful tune parading in my spirit. It became alive in praise and worship to You, oh Lord, Most High. While I am not musically talented to release what I hear, I thank You for Your Holy Spirit that allows me to hear Your music.

Help me, Lord, to rise above fear and doubt about my ability and become so free that I will make public what You have planted in my heart.

Let the music flow, dear Lord. Let the Spirit make the song, the melody, and the praise come alive with joy. For it is in Your joy that we find strength. Hallelujah! I want the words to flow through my mouth into Your ears as a sweet sound and into the hearts of others, tickling them with Your joy. With these songs, I magnify, exalt, and adore You. Anoint these songs to bring lives together and connect people to Your will.

Father, I open my inner self to Your musical notations and characters so that my senses can be flooded with Your praise and Your music—Your heavenly symphony. I am ready to go to a higher level of serving You through song, Lord—another realm of intimacy!

Allow me to hear, sing, and affect the hearts of others with Your music.

*...Sing unto the Lord a new song, and His
praise in the congregation of saints*
(Psalm 149:1).

*...I will declare Thy name unto my brethren, in the
midst of the church will I sing praise unto Thee*
(Hebrews 2:12).

*And be not drunk with wine, wherein is excess; but
be filled with the Spirit; speaking to yourselves in
psalms and hymns and spiritual songs, singing
and making melody in your heart to the Lord*
(Ephesians 5:18-19).

# PRAYER FOR BEAUTY

There is so much ugliness around, so much unkindness in our lives, and so much meanness in our relationships. I must find a way to experience Your beauty. The world's idea of beauty overwhelms me: I don't have the perfect skin, a shapely physique, the "right" skin color, the "right" length of hair, the "right" height, and all the other "right" things they say constitute a beautiful person.

Lord, strengthen me to look beyond the flesh and to seek the inner beauty and not limit myself to the obvious. Though things are sometimes beautiful on the outside, they may be awfully grotesque on the inside. There are those who appear to be sweet and kind initially, but turn out to be vicious and uncaring later on.

I don't want this to be my testimony, so Lord, help me to reach out to embrace Your Word. Help me to stay in Your presence and to live in true beauty.

Teach me to look far beyond physical appearances. Help me to see the undiscovered truth. Guide me to walk in the beauty of holiness and cause me to hear the pure *splendor* of Your will. I want true beauty. Remove the ugly sight and bring forth the appealing presence.

*To appoint unto them that mourn in Zion,*
*to give unto them beauty for ashes...*
(Isaiah 61:3).

*... for praise is comely for the upright*
(Psalm 33:1).

*One thing I have desired of the Lord, that will I seek: that I*
*may dwell in the house of the Lord all the days of my life, to*
*behold the beauty of the Lord, and to inquire in His temple*
(Psalm 27:4 NKJV).

# PRAYER FOR WISDOM

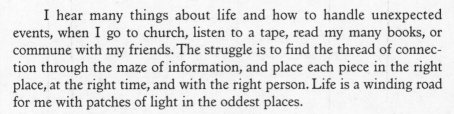

I hear many things about life and how to handle unexpected events, when I go to church, listen to a tape, read my many books, or commune with my friends. The struggle is to find the thread of connection through the maze of information, and place each piece in the right place, at the right time, and with the right person. Life is a winding road for me with patches of light in the oddest places.

Father, You admonish in Your Word that wisdom is the principal thing, so I should get wisdom. O Lord, at this juncture in my life, I do not want to waste time on paths that You have not predestined for me. Open the doors that will lead me to the next predestined path in this journey. There were so many times when I would stagger the wrong way before walking in the right path. But now I realize that those avenues upon which I staggered were not completely wrong, for they were used to help me identify the right way and to get wisdom and understanding.

I now want to hear You differently and move in Your direction quickly. Your wise teaching brings peace, hope, change, and healing in my life. Lord, open my mind to receive the nuggets of godly wisdom that will elevate my mind and shift me into a purer thought life. I am ready to receive from the omniscient God. My God, you are too wise to make a mistake, too kind to send me down crooked paths that lead to desolation, and too loving to leave me to my own devices. Speak, Lord, and I'll do what You say. Direct me, and I'll follow. Glory to God!

*...Blessed be the Lord God of Israel, that made heaven
and earth, who hath given to David the king a wise
son, endued with prudence and understanding...*
(2 Chronicles 2:12).

*Whence then cometh wisdom? and where is the
place of understanding?...God understandeth the
way thereof, and He knoweth the place thereof*
(Job 28:20,23).

*And unto man He said, Behold, the fear of the Lord,
that is wisdom; and to depart from evil is understanding*
(Job 28:28).

# PRAYER FOR MY TRUST LEVEL

Lord, You are asking me to trust someone who has failed me, and the situation doesn't look like it will ever change. It's so hard to trust them. I need proof—I need assurance that they will not disappoint me again—I need information. You seem to ask me to trust earnestly when there is total darkness.

Why do You make it so hard for me to decide, by giving me little or no information? The information You have given is in direct conflict with my reality. I know that You have proven Yourself in the past—I have numerous testimonies of Your faithfulness and power. There is absolutely no reason to doubt Your ability to deliver me out of any gloomy circumstance. There is no doubt that You will not only change me, but also the person I am challenged to trust. I am certain You will fix everything according to Your eternal purpose, but Lord, this route seems hopeless.

Please help me not to trust my senses or my logic. They get in the way of me trusting You, who will stabilize my faith, enrich my understanding, and enhance my maturity. In this experience, show me how to see You even when it's dark. Thank You, Lord, for clarity and for the entrance of light. Amen.

*Oh that I were as in months past, as in the days when God preserved me; when His candle shined upon my head, and when by His light I walked through darkness (Job 29:2-3).*

*In God I will praise His word, in God I have put my trust; I will not fear what flesh can do unto me (Psalm 56:4).*

*The entrance of Thy words giveth light; it giveth understanding to the simple (Psalm 119:130).*

# PRAYER TO DEFEAT THE CYCLE OF "SAMENESS"

What do I do when the walls close in and when the air seems stale and my life is on hold? All I can do is pray for change—any kind of change that will help to break the monotony that seems to rule in my life. I want something new and fresh...something different and exciting. I want enchantment in my life. But no matter how I pray, my prayers seem to bounce back into my ear. I want action. I want movement. I want a more colorful life.

After much agony, I conclude that there must be something to learn in my "sameness." I want You to unveil it to me and stifle the anxiety.

Is there a calm in the midst of this cycle? Are there sights to see and to grow familiar with in this rotation of "sameness"? Help me, Lord, to see it, hear it, and touch it. Though I don't see it, I know that beyond this place of stale frustration, there is a greater place of fresh inspiration. I will flow with my familiar, until the circle is broken. Thank You, Lord, for the wisdom to rest in "sameness"! Amen.

*Wait on the Lord: be of good courage, and He shall*
*strengthen thine heart: wait, I say, on the Lord*
(Psalm 27:14).

*The Lord grant you that ye may find rest,*
*each of you in the house...*
(Ruth 1:9).

*There remaineth therefore a rest to the people of God*
(Hebrews 4:9).

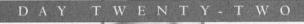

# PRAYER AND WARFARE

Lord, today I offer up thunderous praise against the strategy and intentions of the enemy. The attack against me has been fierce, Lord! It feels as if my strength has been weakened, but I rose up this morning with new vigor and refreshed commitment. This day I declare and decree that no weapon formed against me shall prosper.

I will command with the words of the "Scriptural Meditations"! The words are my two-edged sword to pierce through the darkness the enemy uses to blanket my life. I will be steadfast in my conviction and determination as were Abraham, Esther, and Peter. I will see the plan of the enemy thwarted before my very eyes.

But the Warrior God—Jehovah—He will fight for me and through me. I will gain the victory completely. Glory to God! Hallelujah!

*And when he had consulted with the people, he appointed
singers unto the Lord, and that should praise the beauty of
holiness, as they went out before the army, and to say,
Praise the Lord; for His mercy endureth for ever*
(2 Chronicles 20:21).

*Behold, I give unto you power to tread on serpents
and scorpions, and over all the power of the enemy:
and nothing shall by any means hurt you*
(Luke 10:19).

*...for we are not ignorant of* [satan's] *devices*
(2 Corinthians 2:11).

# PRAYER FOR STAMINA

The pace of my life is very unstable. You stated in Your Word that a double-minded person is unstable in everything, and this person will not receive from You. With this in mind, I know why my blessings are being held back. I am struggling with consistency in everything. I am easily bored, easily distracted, easily frustrated, and easily misdirected.

When will I gain control of my scattered emotions and wandering eyes? I don't know why I am so confused and my attention span is so short. I don't know why I am so easily stimulated by garbage. I have talent, creativity, intelligence, and resources. But Lord, it doesn't seem as though I can pull them all together to make my life meaningful.

My desire to break out into a place of discipline, structure, order, and freedom of accomplishment is a burning aspiration. Grant me the will to make the dreams that You have given me come to pass. Help me to focus on my goals and walk steadily in my destined path. I am open to Your correction, Your guidance, and Your help. I sit in Your presence for this mighty impartation into my being. Bless You, O my Lord!

*A double minded man is unstable in all his ways*
(James 1:8).

*Thou wilt keep him in perfect peace, whose mind is
stayed on Thee: because he trusteth in Thee*
(Isaiah 26:3).

*For the gifts and calling of God are without repentance*
(Romans 11:29).

# PRAYER FOR MY LOVED ONE IN PRISON

Yes, I have helped so many others in their trials. Yes, I have seen Your deliverance in their lives. Yes, I have watched You perform miracles when I prayed for so many others. But I am baffled every time I see my own family member still in prison chains while others go free.

I am not suggesting that I am so special that I should be exempted from negative experiences, Lord; I just ask You for the grace to endure the humiliation and challenge of my family member in prison.

It hurts to see my loved one bound, controlled, used, abused, and degraded behind prison bars. It is not only a physical enclosure, but also emotional bondage. It is hard, at times, to visit the place of entrapment.

Only You, oh merciful Father, can free my loved one from these fetters of spiritual and emotional bondage. Please take the chain of darkness off their mind. Release their will into Your will so that true power and enlightenment can penetrate the soul.

I am not asking You to simply move them from a physical state, but move them into a spiritual life. This will bring them closer to Your purpose for them and the blessedness of communion with You. I am confident that You will hear this prayer and intervene beyond the judicial system and correctional facility. I believe You, Lord. And I praise You in advance for the miraculous release!

*Naked, and ye clothed Me: I was sick, and ye
visited Me: I was in prison, and ye came unto Me*
(Matthew 25:36).

*The Spirit of the Lord God  is upon Me; because the
Lord hath anointed Me to preach good tidings unto
the meek; He hath sent Me to bind up the brokenhearted, to proclaim liberty to the captives, and the
opening of the prison to them that are bound*
(Isaiah 61:1).

*And at midnight Paul and Silas prayed, and sang praises
unto God: and the prisoners heard them. And suddenly
there was a great earthquake, so that the foundations of
the prison were shaken: and immediately all the doors
were opened, and every one's bands were loosed*
(Acts 16:25-26).

# PRAYER TO COMMUNICATE WITH SOMEONE WHO IS A NONCOMMUNICATOR

I am so frustrated with problems of communication with people who are just closed. They are "one-sentence" people. Talking to them is like pulling teeth. Obviously, the level of trust that it takes to communicate freely is not there. I feel totally immobilized, because I like to communicate, relating to and reaching people through words, thoughts, and ideas.

Please give me the grace to be patient and to understand their position. Likewise, give them the grace also to be free to speak their minds, their hearts, and their feelings. This would make it so much easier to love them, understand them, and connect with them. I praise You in advance for the change in our communication.

*A word fitly spoken is like apples of gold in pictures of silver*
(Proverbs 25:11).

*Iron sharpeneth iron; so a man sharpeneth*
*the countenance of his friend*
(Proverbs 27:17).

*As in water face answereth to face,*
*so the heart of man to man*
(Proverbs 27:19).

*The words of the wise are as goads, and as nails fastened by*
*the masters of assemblies, which are given from one shepherd*
(Ecclesiastes 12:11).

# PRAYER FROM A CAREGIVER

Lord, my loved one is incapacitated and cannot make decisions for their health and their future. I have decided crucial medical, personal, and physical choices on their behalf for the betterment of their lives. This is so heavy for me right now.

I feel alone; I feel insufficient; I feel insecure and desperate. Give me the right people to guide me, who understand my loved one's purpose and destiny. Lord, lift the spirit of panic and fright so that I can think clearly. You said in Your Word that You have not given me the spirit of fear, but You have given me a disciplined and sobered mind.

I want to walk through this with Your wisdom and guidance. I want to display my caregiving with confidence and kindness. Release Your presence, Your people, and Your resources so that this experience will bring peace to all and glory to You. Thank You, Lord!

*And Joseph nourished his father, and his brethren, and all his father's household, with bread, according to their families* (Genesis 47:12).

*And David went thence to Mizpeh of Moab: and he said unto the king of Moab, Let my father and my mother, I pray thee, come forth, and be with you, till I know what God will do for me. And he brought them before the king of Moab: and they dwelt with him all the while that David was in the hold* (1 Samuel 22:3-4).

*Now there stood by the cross of Jesus His mother, and His mother's sister, Mary the wife of Cleophas, and Mary Magdalene. When Jesus therefore saw His mother, and the disciple standing by, whom He loved, He saith unto His mother, Woman, behold thy son! Then saith He to the disciple, Behold thy mother! And from that hour that disciple took her unto his own home* (John 19:25-27).

# PRAYER AGAINST HIDING

Why do I hide and run from people so readily? Why do I expect the worst when I encounter confrontations? Why would I rather withdraw and leave the room than to speak my mind clearly and boldly? These are the questions that plague me on my night's bed and in my quiet moments.

I would like to know what it feels like to face anyone and anything without the worry of being devastated by a negative response. I just want to live outside of the rejection box.

This box has confined and restrained me far too long. I want to escape as a bird out of the inner entrapment. Free me, Lord, so that I will not be overly concerned about people's acceptance or rejection of me. Thank You, Lord!

*The Lord is my light and my salvation; whom shall I fear?*
*the Lord is the strength of my life; of whom shall I be afraid?*
*When the wicked, even mine enemies and my foes, came*
*upon me to eat up my flesh, they stumbled and fell. Though*
*an host should encamp against me, my heart shall not fear:*
*though war should rise against me, in this will I be confident*
(Psalm 27:1-3).

*The fear of man bringeth a snare: but whoso*
*putteth his trust in the Lord shall be safe*
(Proverbs 29:25).

*I, even I, am He that comforteth you: who art thou, that*
*thou shouldest be afraid of a man that shall die, and of the*
*son of man which shall be made as grass; and forgettest the*
*Lord thy maker, that hath stretched forth the heavens, and*
*laid the foundations of the earth; and hast feared continually*
*every day because of the fury of the oppressor, as if he were*
*ready to destroy? and where is the fury of the oppressor?*
(Isaiah 51:12-13)

*So that we may boldly say, The Lord is my helper,*
*and I will not fear what man shall do unto me*
(Hebrews 13:6).

# PRAYER FROM A COLLEGE STUDENT

Lord, I have never been away from home before and I am petri-fied. I bragged so much, when I graduated from high school, about how ready I was to leave home. I saw myself living without parental control and interference. I dreamed of talking on the phone as much as I wanted, staying out as long as I wanted, and studying whenever I thought necessary...

I am now away from home and have the freedom to do all these things, but the freedom exposes weaknesses that I have never dealt with before. I did not know that I was a follower instead of a leader. I did not know that sex was a must if I wanted to be with the "in" crowd. I did not know that independence would carry such a price. I am shaking because I can't hide behind my parents and their protection of me. I am being seen now for who I really am.

Lord, I was raised in church, but now I need to be the Church from the inside out. I cannot make it through this experience deceitfully. I have nowhere to hide. If I hang out late, it will show up immediately in my grades. If I choose the wrong friends, I will soon be caught up in immorality. If I fail to take a stand for You, I will stand for anything against You.

Lord, this is not about Mom, Dad, or the church members, but this is about You and me. I need You to empower me to become the better me. I don't want to be a college dropout, but a spiritual drop-in. I want to drop into the world with my faith, my talent, my hopes, my dreams, and my knowledge. Help me, Lord!

*Wherewithal shall a young man cleanse his way?*
*by taking heed thereto according to Thy word*
(Psalm 119:9).

*Rejoice, O young man, in thy youth; and let thy heart*
*cheer thee in the days of thy youth, and walk in the ways*
*of thine heart, and in the sight of thine eyes: but know thou,*
*that for all these things God will bring thee into judgment*
(Ecclesiastes 11:9).

*Let no man despise thy youth; but be thou an*
*example of the believers, in word, in conversation,*
*in charity, in spirit, in faith, in purity*
(1 Timothy 4:12).

*Young men likewise exhort to be sober minded. In all*
*things showing thyself a pattern of good works: in*
*doctrine showing uncorruptness, gravity, sincerity*
(Titus 2:6-7).

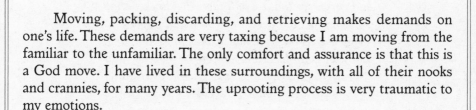

# PRAYER FROM ONE
# WHO IS RELOCATING

Moving, packing, discarding, and retrieving makes demands on one's life. These demands are very taxing because I am moving from the familiar to the unfamiliar. The only comfort and assurance is that this is a God move. I have lived in these surroundings, with all of their nooks and crannies, for many years. The uprooting process is very traumatic to my emotions.

Should I leave this or that? Should I throw away this or keep that? Should I give away this or sell that? This takes so much energy that my anticipation of newness wears thin.

Give me the grace to know that where I am cannot be compared to where I am going. I have to make new friends. I have to find the nearest pharmacy and grocery store. I have to find my way to and from my home. This is all new. I am asking You for the ability to embrace the new place, the new life, and the new journey. Thank You, Lord!

*Now the Lord had said unto Abram, Get thee out
of thy country, and from thy kindred, and from thy
father's house, unto a land that I will show thee:
and I will make of thee a great nation, and I will
bless thee, and make thy name great; and thou shalt
be a blessing: and I will bless them that bless thee,
and curse him that curseth thee: and in thee shall
all families of the earth be blessed. So Abram
departed, as the Lord had spoken unto him; and
Lot went with him: and Abram was seventy and
five years old when he departed out of Haran*
(Genesis 12:1-4).

*As an eagle stirreth up her nest, fluttereth over her
young, spreadeth abroad her wings, taketh them,
beareth them on her wings: so the Lord alone did
lead him, and there was no strange god with him*
(Deuteronomy 32:11-12).

*Thou leddest Thy people like a flock
by the hand of Moses and Aaron*
(Psalm 77:20).

*Brethren, I count not myself to have apprehended:
but this one thing I do, forgetting those things which
are behind, and reaching forth unto those things
which are before, I press toward the mark for the
prize of the high calling of God in Christ Jesus*
(Philippians 3:13-14).

# PRAYER OF DISCOVERY

I am walking so close to You that each day is a day of new experiences. I started out this day with worship and conversation around Your Word. I didn't expect such a burst of inspiration, such a flood of warm feelings, and such a fullness of Your presence.

Please receive my praise and accept my gratitude, because I am gliding through a journey that broadens my views and opens my heart. Lord, continue to work Your work in me and through me. Continue to lift my vision and guide my expectations.

Oh, what newness; oh, what freshness; and oh, what lightness! I am having a time with You, Lord, which I longed for. Yes! This is how one walks in anointing and power. Glory be to God!

*And He hath put a new song in my mouth,*
*even praise unto our God: many shall see it,*
*and fear, and shall trust in the Lord*
(Psalm 40:3).

*Behold, the former things are come to pass, and new*
*things do I declare: before they spring forth I tell you of*
*them. Sing unto the Lord a new song, and His praise*
*from the end of the earth, ye that go down to the sea, and*
*all that is therein; the isles, and the inhabitants thereof*
(Isaiah 42:9-10).

*It is of the Lord's mercies that we are not consumed,*
*because His compassions fail not. They are new*
*every morning: great is Thy faithfulness*
(Lamentations 3:22-23).

# PRAYER AGAINST NEGATIVE FEAR

Dear God, You gave me this alert mechanism called fear to warn me about the unpleasantness in my life. I appreciate the sharp pain in my chest that indicates ill health. I thank You for the dreams and premonitions that have prepared me for the shifts and turns on my journey.

But, I know You do not want me to live with the *spirit of fear*, which paralyzes me and hinders my mobility. I become so gripped with the feeling of helplessness that I can't pray, hope, or think. There are times when You want me to feel my dependency on You, more than other times. There are times when You want me to just stand still and believe You without applying effort to the plan. This immobilization, however, is not waiting or trusting time, but fearing and anxiety time.

My heart beats louder, my voice cracks, my pupils dilate, and my palms perspire. I am sure there are other effects this apprehension has on my mind and body that I am not aware of. This is not of You. You did not give me this spirit. I reject it from my system, mind, and body. I will trust You, lean on You, and hold on to Your Word. I feel Your presence warming and soothing my nerves right now. This is the beginning of a new way of thinking and living. Thank You, Lord, for a life without negative fear!

*After these things the word of the Lord came unto
Abram in a vision, saying, Fear not, Abram: I am
thy shield, and thy exceeding great reward*
(Genesis 15:1).

*O Zion, that bringest good tidings, get thee up into the high
mountain; O Jerusalem, that bringest good tidings, lift
up thy voice with strength; lift it up, be not afraid; say
unto the cities of Judah, Behold your God!*
(Isaiah 40:9)

*For God hath not given us the spirit of fear; but
of power, and of love, and of a sound mind*
(2 Timothy 1:7).

# PRAYER FOR DAILY LIGHTHEARTEDNESS

I want to sing a song that brings back sweet flavor to my soul. How can I live with lightness and freedom, in spite of the burdens and troubles that come to dwell in my space? Lightheartedness is what I want, God, because there is no problem that You cannot solve and no mountain that You cannot remove.

I know Your power. I want to get to the place where I laugh at the devil and his devices at the onset of the challenge. I want my heart to ring with the melody of joy and my tongue to roll with the glee of happiness. This is the place of true confidence. This is life of complete trust. I can be light because I know You will take care of me. Give me this light spirit of the soul, Lord, and my spirit will leap with hilarity. Thank You, Lord—Ha, Ha, Ha!

*Then he said unto them, Go your way, eat the fat, and drink the sweet, and send portions unto them for whom nothing is prepared: for this day is holy unto our Lord: neither be ye sorry; for the joy of the Lord is your strength*
(Nehemiah 8:10).

*Then was our mouth filled with laughter, and our tongue with singing: then said they among the heathen, The Lord hath done great things for them*
(Psalm 126:2).

*Rejoice in the Lord always: and again I say, Rejoice*
(Philippians 4:4).

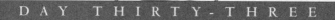

# PRAYER FOR EMOTIONAL SPACE

Situations and people can torment me so that I need a hiding place. It is so hard at times to find seclusion or downtime, in order to recoup from the blows, disappointments, and disillusionments I encounter periodically. This place is a place of refuge, a place of healing, and a place of quiet rest. This is what I need every now and then.

Help me to know when I must distance myself in order to experience myself in Your divine presence. You love me, You care for me, and You will sustain me. Your arms are strong enough to bear me up in my feeble times; therefore, I cherish the moments that I can be tenderly nurtured and refreshed by You.

There are some friends, family members, and associates who create a toxic atmosphere that seeks to poison my whole existence. I crave for Your presence when the air becomes polluted with hate, anger, envy, jealousy, and unkindness. Show me the escape routes so that I can hide under the shadow of Your wings and be safe. You are my security, O Lord!

*Keep me as the apple of the eye, hide me under the*
*shadow of Thy wings, from the wicked that oppress*
*me, from my deadly enemies, who compass me about*
(Psalm 17:8-9).

*And I said, Oh that I had wings like a dove!*
*for then would I fly away, and be at rest*
(Psalm 55:6).

*For thou hast been a strength to the poor, a strength*
*to the needy in his distress, a refuge from the storm,*
*a shadow from the heat, when the blast of the*
*terrible ones is as a storm against the wall*
(Isaiah 25:4).

# PRAYER FROM THE WEARY MIND

Rocks have replaced my brain cells. I feel so heavy that I don't have the strength to hold or release my thoughts. My eyelids are drooped and my eyebrows are wrinkled with tight folds. It is impossible to think of anything other than my depleted mind and weary heart.

So many times I get a lift, especially in praise and worship; but when I leave church, the weights and cares of life burden me down so heavily. I know that this is a momentary experience, which will lead to a greater appreciation of Your joy, peace, and power. In the meantime, however, I ask Your divine intervention upon my unending weariness and into my lingering dreariness.

I need a mighty move and a right-now miracle. The lifting of this heaviness will give me back the courage and stamina to love and praise You the more. I want to walk lightly and move easily into Your presence throughout this season. Grant it, Lord Jesus!

*Thou, O God, didst send a plentiful rain, whereby Thou
didst confirm Thine inheritance, when it was weary*
(Psalm 68:9).

*Even the youths shall faint and be weary, and the
young men shall utterly fall: but they that wait upon
the Lord shall renew their strength; they shall mount
up with wings as eagles; they shall run, and not be
weary; and they shall walk, and not faint*
(Isaiah 40:30-31).

*And let us not be weary in well doing: for in
due season we shall reap, if we faint not*
(Galatians 6:9).

*And be renewed in the spirit of your mind*
(Ephesians 4:23).

# PRAYER AGAINST FRUSTRATION

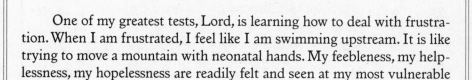

One of my greatest tests, Lord, is learning how to deal with frustration. When I am frustrated, I feel like I am swimming upstream. It is like trying to move a mountain with neonatal hands. My feebleness, my helplessness, my hopelessness are readily felt and seen at my most vulnerable moments.

These moments make me feel naked, handicapped, and useless. *What should I do?* becomes the question. The answer, however, seems so far away. I need my frustration level to be reduced to a point where I can grab myself back before I get too stressed out. How do I do that Lord? Where do I go?

The only things I can think about are meditation, listening to music, or calling a prayerful friend. If these things are not possible, I will just stop everything, close my eyes, and wait on You. I know You will speak a word that will dispel my fears and anxiety. Help me, Lord, to respond to You differently in my time of frustration. Bless You, Lord!

*Rest in the Lord, and wait patiently for Him: fret not thyself because of him who prospereth in his way, because of the man who bringeth wicked devices to pass*
(Psalm 37:7).

*Better is the end of a thing than the beginning thereof: and the patient in spirit is better than the proud in spirit. Be not hasty in thy spirit to be angry: for anger resteth in the bosom of fools*
(Ecclesiastes 7:8-9).

*In your patience possess ye your souls*
(Luke 21:19).

*That ye might walk worthy of the Lord unto all pleasing, being fruitful in every good work, and increasing in the knowledge of God; strengthened with all might, according to His glorious power, unto all patience and longsuffering with joyfulness*
(Colossians 1:10-11).

# PRAYER AGAINST
# SEPARATION ANXIETY

One of the hardest things for me is saying good-bye. I don't know how others handle it, but I really go through a lot of changes in my emotions.

Knowing someone or being familiar with something creates a strong bond with me. I become deeply attached, whether it is a positive or negative attachment. Lord, You have had to break me out of some addictive attachments over the years. I am so grateful that the spirit of codependency has been lifted from me.

Please help me deal with the separation of friends and even enemies. I want to part with a healthy spirit. It is normal to mourn, grieve, and sense loss. But I take myself through severe changes—overeating, oversleeping, withdrawing, denying, and complaining. This is not a reflection of Your grace and power. I should shed tears when I separate from something or someone special, but I should not exemplify such destructive behaviors.

I want to be free to go in and out of life's changes without a feeling of desperation or abandonment. Thank You, Lord, for this freedom, in Jesus' name!

*...lo, I am with you always, even*
*unto the end of the world. Amen*
(Matthew 28:20).

*Who shall separate us from the love of Christ?*
*shall tribulation, or distress, or persecution, or*
*famine, or nakedness, or peril, or sword?  As it is*
*written, For Thy sake we are killed all the day long;*
*we are accounted as sheep for the slaughter. Nay,*
*in all these things we are more than conquerors*
*through Him that loved us.  For I am persuaded,*
*that neither death, nor life, nor angels, nor*
*principalities, nor powers, nor things present,*
*nor things to come, nor height, nor depth, nor any*
*other creature, shall be able to separate us from*
*the love of God, which is in Christ Jesus our Lord*
(Romans 8:35-39).

*Let your conversation be without covetousness; and be*
*content with such things as ye have: for He hath said,*
*I will never leave thee, nor forsake thee*
(Hebrews 13:5).

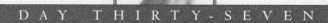

# PRAYER AGAINST THE SPIRIT OF SUICIDE

How can I explain this to You, Lord? Why should I explain it, when You know everything? The feeling of total escape through the thought of suicide brings a strange kind of comfort. I feel relieved of the pressure, the responsibility, and the stress. It is so much easier to see myself flying away as a bird to heights unknown.

The depression sets in when I realize that I am not a bird and that life still goes on. The courage to take my life is a constant challenge, but a continual thought. I have looked at the pill bottle, examined the razor's edge, and located the nearest bridge. It is only the prayers of family and friends that have sustained me during the bouts of suicidal tendencies.

I want out of this death-wish journey. I want to look at life differently with a passion to live it. Please hear my cry and intervene on my behalf. Hold my hand, Lord, lest I fall. Keep my mind, Lord, when I call. Lift my heart, Lord, through it all. If You do these things, then I can live. Thank You! Thank You! Thank You, Lord!

*I shall not die, but live, and declare the works of
the Lord. The Lord hath chastened me sore:
but He hath not given me over unto death*
(Psalm 118:17-18).

*Where can I go from Your Spirit? Where can I flee from Your
presence? If I go up to the heavens, You are there; if I make
my bed in the depths, You are there. If I rise on the wings of
the dawn, if I settle on the far side of the sea, even there Your
hand will guide me, Your right hand will hold me fast*
(Psalm 139:7-10 NIV).

*To appoint unto them that mourn in Zion, to give
unto them beauty for ashes, the oil of joy for mourning,
the garment of praise for the spirit of heaviness; that
they might be called trees of righteousness, the planting
of the Lord, that He might be glorified*
(Isaiah 61:3).

*These things I have spoken unto you, that in Me ye
might have peace. In the world ye shall have tribulation:
but be of good cheer; I have overcome the world*
(John 16:33).

# PRAYER TO CROSS OVER

Every now and then I get to this place, Jesus, where I must go to the other side. I know that life is about change, and change is about life. Yet, when I have to cross over to the new, the unfamiliar, and the different, I become almost frantic and desperate.

There is no going back to the old. I must cross over, but I procrastinate and linger at the edge. I touch the border and draw back. I see the opening and let go of the entrance. I know the time is now, but I hold on to the *later*.

Give me the courage to take this breath and this step into the inevitability of Your will. Lord, I close my eyes tight, clench my fists hard, and cross over in Your name. I will make it, because You will carry me over. Thank You, Lord!

*And* [Jacob] *rose up that night, and took his two
wives, and his two womenservants, and his eleven
sons, and passed over the ford Jabbok*
(Genesis 32:22).

*And the Lord said unto Moses, Wherefore criest thou unto
Me? speak unto the children of Israel, that they go forward*
(Exodus 14:15).

*And he took the mantle of Elijah that fell from him,
and smote the waters, and said, Where is the Lord
God of Elijah? and when he also had smitten the waters,
they parted hither and thither: and Elisha went over*
(2 Kings 2:14).

*And he went a little farther, and fell on his face, and
prayed, saying, O my Father, if it be possible, let this cup
pass from me: nevertheless not as I will, but as thou wilt*
(Matthew 26:39).

# PRAYER AGAINST AVOIDANCE

Running, running, running. It's what I do well, especially when I feel overwhelmed and challenged. If the subject is sticky, I clam up. If the issue is about my issues, I shut down. If truth must be spoken, I ramble on and on. I just can't deal with confrontation or direct approach to a matter. I want it smooth, easy, and couched in laughter and playfulness.

Life, however, cannot be avoided. Truth must not be skirted. Issues will not disappear without resolve. I need help in my passive/aggressive response to life. I am passive, because I won't deal up front. I am aggressive because I handle it only when I am forced to. I want out of this psychological prison. You said if I know truth, speak truth, and live truth, I would be free. Please help me to walk in the spirit of freedom and not avoidance. Thank You, Jesus!

*And they heard the voice of the Lord God walking in the garden in the cool of the day: and Adam and his wife hid themselves from the presence of the Lord God amongst the trees of the garden (Genesis 3:8).*

*I will not be afraid of ten thousands of people, that have set themselves against me round about (Psalm 3:6).*

*Though an host should encamp against me, my heart shall not fear: though war should rise against me, in this will I be confident (Psalm 27:3)*

*And ye shall know the truth, and the truth shall make you free (John 8:32).*

# PRAYER FOR THE "YES"

I can remember the times of the "terrible twos" and the "terrible threes" attitude in my walk with You, Lord. I said "no" to everything, before I even understood it. I am a victim of my Adamic nature. This will and flesh of mine want what they want and nothing else. I thrive on the cravings of my desires and seek to fulfill them with cheap gratifications that are very short-lived.

Please, dear God, help me to satisfy the longings of my soul with Your Word, Your presence, and Your will. This, of course, is easier said than done. But I am committed to being one of Your children who bring glory to Your name and peace to my heart. I will begin by changing my verbal response to Your requests. I will now say "yes" more readily than saying "no." If I should say "no" first, then I will speedily adjust my lips and heart to say, "Yes, Lord."

*Now therefore, if ye will obey my voice indeed, and
keep My covenant, then ye shall be a peculiar treasure
unto Me above all people: for all the earth is mine*
(Exodus 19:5).

*But what think ye? A certain man had two sons;
and he came to the first, and said, Son, go work today
in my vineyard. He answered and said, I will not: but
afterward he repented, and went. And he came to the
second, and said likewise. And he answered and said,
I go, sir: and went not. Whether of them twain did the
will of his father? They say unto him, The first*
(Matthew 21:28-31a).

*Wherefore, my beloved, as ye have always obeyed,
not as in my presence only, but now much more
in my absence, work out your own salvation with
fear and trembling. For it is God which worketh in
you both to will and to do of His good pleasure*
(Philippians 2:12-13).

# PRAYER FOR RECOVERY

Addictions and obsessive habits have ruled my emotions and behavior for years. It is not just the addictions to alcohol or drugs that have manipulated my existence; it has also been addictions of the hidden, dark emotions of my mind that have caused me to look to substances and abuse these substances.

I yearned for love and was given hate. I reached for acceptance and received rejection. I tried to please everyone and was criticized by many. I went from super high on false love to super low on real life. I turned inward but found no solace or comfort. However, one day, You found me, Lord, and I have never been the same.

I am now discovering more addictions. I stopped drugs, but I still have a craving for attention, even the wrong kinds of attention. My prayer today is for wholeness, so that nothing drives me so hard that it interferes with my love for You. Balance me, heal me, cover and sustain me. I want to walk in full recovery of my heart, soul, mind, and body. I will praise You, love You, obey You, and worship until this recovery is complete.

*O Lord, by these things men live, and in all these things is the life of my spirit: so wilt thou recover me, and make me to live* (Isaiah 38:16).

*But when Jesus heard that, He said unto them, They that be whole need not a physician, but they that are sick* (Matthew 9:12).

*How God anointed Jesus of Nazareth with the Holy Ghost and with power: who went about doing good, and healing all that were oppressed of the devil; for God was with Him* (Acts 10:38).

# PRAYER FROM THE SOUL

Lord, I feel like I am going through the "valley of the shadow of death" (Ps. 23:4). My soul feels dark and dry. It seems as if I am sinking deeper and deeper into an abysmal state.

I was faced with an unexpected disappointment from someone really close. Their spirit lanced into the fibers of my soul with a reality that was almost unbearable. Pain and torment suctioned my heart and spirit into a tunnel of unending despair.

I see myself falling without the ability to catch myself back. Please, Lord, rescue me, before the day breaks—before the day breaks me! Send help from Heaven, because You are able to keep me from plummeting downward. Shift me to an upward move, and I will praise You as I go higher and higher.

*For Thou wilt not leave my soul in hell; neither wilt*
*Thou suffer Thine Holy One to see corruption*
(Psalm 16:10)

*To deliver their soul from death, and to keep them*
*alive in famine. Our soul waiteth for the Lord:*
*He is our help and our shield*
(Psalm 33:19-20)

*Why art thou cast down, O my soul? and why art thou*
*disquieted in me? hope thou in God: for I shall yet praise*
*Him for the help of His countenance....Why art thou*
*cast down, O my soul? and why art thou disquieted*
*within me? hope thou in God: for I shall yet praise Him,*
*who is the health of my countenance, and my God*
(Psalm 42:5,11).

# PRAYER FROM
# A CLEAR MIND

*Thank You! Thank You! Thank You, Lord!* It is amazing how I have blamed everyone else for my challenges, struggles, and failures. It is embarrassing to remember how I have attacked others because I couldn't truly see myself.

All the difficulties that I recently faced were designed to bring me to a central truth in my life. This truth is that I need to change, and it takes pressure to change my character. I thought I was fine and that my faults weren't so bad.

It took You, Lord, to burst open my heart and unveil my eyes so that I could have a clear mind. This test was positioned in my way to carry me closer to Your heart and bring me closer to my greater self. *Thank You, Lord!*

*Thus my heart was grieved, and I was pricked in my reins.*
*So foolish was I, and ignorant: I was as a beast before*
*Thee. Nevertheless I am continually with Thee: Thou*
*hast holden me by my right hand. Thou shalt guide me*
*with Thy counsel, and afterward receive me to glory*
(Psalm 73:21-24).

*Open Thou mine eyes, that I may*
*behold wondrous things out of Thy law*
(Psalm 119:18).

*But blessed are your eyes, for they see:*
*and your ears, for they hear*
(Matthew 13:16).

*For God, who commanded the light to shine out of darkness,*
*hath shined in our hearts, to give the light of the knowledge*
*of the glory of God in the face of Jesus Christ*
(2 Corinthians 4:6).

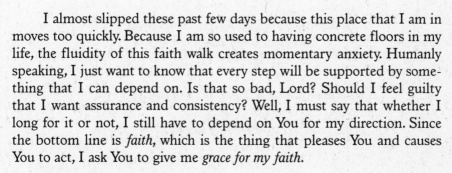

# PRAYER FROM A FLUID PLACE

I almost slipped these past few days because this place that I am in moves too quickly. Because I am so used to having concrete floors in my life, the fluidity of this faith walk creates momentary anxiety. Humanly speaking, I just want to know that every step will be supported by something that I can depend on. Is that so bad, Lord? Should I feel guilty that I want assurance and consistency? Well, I must say that whether I long for it or not, I still have to depend on You for my direction. Since the bottom line is *faith*, which is the thing that pleases You and causes You to act, I ask You to give me *grace for my faith*.

With this needed grace, my faith will hold my feet steady in this period of slippery moves. The places may not change, the changes may not be smooth, and my steps may be awkward; but my heart will be steadily beating with Your grace and Word. I trust You, Lord, for this experience, in Jesus' name. Amen.

*Behold, his soul which is lifted up is not upright
in him: but the just shall live by his faith*
(Habakkuk 2:4).

*For we walk by faith, not by sight*
(2 Corinthians 5:7).

*Now faith is the substance of things hoped for,
the evidence of things not seen*
(Hebrews 11:1).

*But without faith it is impossible to please Him: for he
that cometh to God must believe that He is, and that He
is a rewarder of them that diligently seek Him*
(Hebrews 11:6).

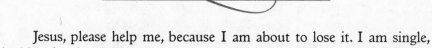

# PRAYER FOR THE TRUE MEANING OF DATING

Jesus, please help me, because I am about to lose it. I am single, looking for the right mate. I know that the single life, in and out of the church, can be nothing but pure drudgery. Some go to singles' hangouts and others to Internet dugouts for connections. I just want what You have for me, whether it is friendship or marriage.

My fleshly weakness keeps me in a quandary, because when I date, I end up entertaining my fleshly desires before I even get to know the person. First of all, I can't and don't want to hear anything spiritual when I am being kissed, rubbed, or necked. It is not that I don't love You, Lord Jesus, but I can't hear You when my flesh is being stimulated with heated pleasure. Prayer, the will of God, and righteousness are not on my mind when my desires are being appeased.

It is the morning (or night) after that I ask myself, "Who is this person and do I want to spend the rest of my life with them?" This is so backwards and out of sorts, because their touch, smell, breath, and feel are all over me. When I need another rub or touch, I know just where to go. This is not what I want for the rest of my life.

Most importantly, Lord, I want the "spiritual" and not the "soul" mate who will be my covenant mate for life. If I could just wait and seek to please You in all my ways, leave myself open to Your guidance, and then connect with the person in a godly way, I would be walking in a more complete walk with You.

Teach me how to have good friends, participate in group activities, and refine my character as a person, before I start a self-gratification pursuit with a partner of my choice, instead of Your choice. Please hear my cry, O Lord.

*And Jacob served seven years for Rachel; and they seemed
unto him but a few days, for the love he had to her*
(Genesis 29:20).

*Three things are too wonderful for me; four I do not
understand: the way of an eagle in the sky, the way
of a serpent on a rock, the way of a ship on the high
seas, and the way of a man with a virgin*
(Proverbs 30:18-19 ESV).

*I want you to be free from anxieties. The unmarried man is
anxious about the things of the Lord, how to please the Lord*
(1 Corinthians 7:32 ESV).

*For this is the will of God, even your sanctification, that ye
should abstain from fornication: that every one of you should
know how to possess his vessel in sanctification and honour*
(1 Thesssalonians 4:3-4).

# PRAYER FROM A MOTHER WITH A TODDLER

Busy, busy, busy. That is the story of my toddler's life. Lord, whatever happened to that wonderful, cuddly child resting on my lap or in the crib? It seems as if an electrically-charged motor robot has come forth to terrorize my space.

I have not shifted because I still want a controlled environment. I need time to coordinate my life. Yet, there is this moving creature, pulling, tearing down, and readjusting every place in the house.

Give me the wisdom, grace, patience, and creativity to flow with this stage of exploration in my child's life. I don't want to stifle their curiosity and discovery, but I need to take back a piece of my life so that I can spend some time in Your presence.

Am I a selfish parent? If so, help me! If I am not being too selfish, then show me how to keep my sanity, enjoy my child, and grow in grace.

*Also that day they offered great sacrifices, and*
*rejoiced: for God had made them rejoice with great*
*joy: the wives also and the children rejoiced: so*
*that the joy of Jerusalem was heard even afar off*
(Nehemiah 12:43).

*Out of the mouth of babes and sucklings hast Thou*
*ordained strength because of Thine enemies, that*
*Thou mightest still the enemy and the avenger*
(Psalm 8:2).

*He maketh the barren woman to keep house, and*
*to be a joyful mother of children. Praise ye the Lord*
(Psalm 113:9).

*And when the chief priests and scribes saw the wonderful*
*things that He did, and the children crying in the temple,*
*and saying, Hosanna to the Son of David; they were sore*
*displeased, and said unto Him, Hearest Thou what these say?*
*And Jesus saith unto them, Yea; have ye never read, Out of*
*the mouth of babes and sucklings Thou hast perfected praise?*
(Matthew 21:15-16)

# PRAYER FROM
# ADOPTIVE PARENTS

Whose child is this, Lord? We are the caregivers of this wonderful child—this child who has come to look like us, talk like us, and act more like us every day. We saw the first walk, heard the first words, and celebrated the first bathroom trip.

Thank You, Lord, for the godly transfer of this precious child, who has blessed us to enter spiritually-adopted parenthood. Ever keep us mindful of our privilege to nurture one of Your special gems. Amen.

*And now thy two sons, Ephraim and Manasseh,*
*which were born unto thee in the land of Egypt*
*before I came unto thee into Egypt, are mine;*
*as Reuben and Simeon, they shall be mine*
(Genesis 48:5).

*Therefore shall ye lay up these My words in your heart and*
*in your soul, and bind them for a sign upon your hand, that*
*they may be as frontlets between your eyes. And ye shall*
*teach them your children, speaking of them when thou sittest*
*in thine house, and when thou walkest by the way, when thou*
*liest down, and when thou risest up. And thou shalt write*
*them upon the door posts of thine house, and upon thy gates:*
*that your days may be multiplied, and the days of your*
*children, in the land which the Lord sware unto your fathers*
*to give them, as the days of heaven upon the earth*
(Deuteronomy 11:18-21).

*For ye have not received the spirit of bondage again*
*to fear; but ye have received the Spirit of adoption,*
*whereby we cry, Abba, Father*
(Romans 8:15).

*For ye are all the children of God by faith in Christ Jesus*
(Galatians 3:26).

# PRAYER FOR CONTENTMENT

Lord, the dichotomy of adversity and prosperity can really throw me into a tailspin. Just when I think I have a space of rest and quiet, I find myself in the midst of a storm. For many years, I have been tossed to and fro in my faith walk because I just can't reconcile the extreme differences in these experiences.

I got the new job, but the supervisor hassles me every day. I did get the new car You promised, but the insurance company hiked up my payments. How should I embrace the blessings and the challenges without being totally frustrated?

There is a place called "contentment" that I desire to embrace. It is a place of grace, where I can traffic through adversity and enjoy prosperity within the same space of grace. I want to have a balanced approach to life and hold the reins of my mind in Your presence through it all. Teach me how to be content in all things. Thank You, Lord.

*Not that I speak in respect of want: for I have learned,
in whatsoever state I am, therewith to be content*
(Philippians 4:11).

*And having food and raiment let us be therewith content*
(1 Timothy 6:8).

*Let your conversation be without covetousness; and be
content with such things as ye have: for He hath said,
I will never leave thee, nor forsake thee*
(Hebrews 13:5).

# PRAYER FOR A PURE HEART

I often hurt others with my words, because I have been hurt. I have such strong feelings about my pain and disappointment that I lash out and criticize everyone around me.

When I hear the words that I have spoken in haste, in jest, and in sarcasm, I am ashamed of myself. It is out of the depths of the heart that the mouth speaks. It just flows, without effort and without much thought—words that reflect my heart.

I want to have a clean heart and the right spirit towards myself and others. You did it for David, so please do it for me. Thanks, Lord, in advance.

*Who shall ascend into the hill of the Lord? or who
shall stand in His holy place? He that hath clean
hands, and a pure heart; who hath not lifted up his
soul unto vanity, nor sworn deceitfully*
(Psalm 24:3-4).

*He that loveth pureness of heart, for the grace
of his lips the king shall be his friend*
(Proverbs 22:11).

*Now the end of the commandment is charity out of a pure
heart, and of a good conscience, and of faith unfeigned*
(1 Timothy 1:5).

*Flee also youthful lusts: but follow righteous-
ness, faith, charity, peace, with them that call
on the Lord out of a pure heart*
(2 Timothy 2:22).

*Seeing ye have purified your souls in obeying the truth
through the Spirit unto unfeigned love of the brethren, see
that ye love one another with a pure heart fervently*
(1 Peter 1:22).

# PRAYER FOR MISSIONS

The harvest is ripe, the fields are white, and souls are ready to be brought into the Kingdom of God. I feel the press, the charge, and the passion to reach out to people beyond my borders. They eat differently, speak differently, and even believe differently. Yet, I feel the love of God pulsating in my breast for those who respond to the gospel of Jesus Christ.

I pledge my prayers, my talents, my resources, and my love to saving and caring for God's people. I have to make the trip to these remote countries; and my sisters and brothers who support me, help make the mission, the message, and the ministry possible.

Thank You, Lord, for the connection that makes the mission possible. Send Your Word and Your Spirit to stir others into active service, so that Your light can shine across the world. Send forth laborers, Lord. Send forth caregivers, Lord. Send forth Your love, Lord.

*The Spirit of the Lord God is upon Me; because the Lord hath anointed Me to preach good tidings unto the meek; He hath sent Me to bind up the brokenhearted, to proclaim liberty to the captives, and the opening of the prison to them that are bound*
(Isaiah 61:1).

*Go ye therefore, and teach all nations, baptizing them in the name of the Father, and of the Son, and of the Holy Ghost: teaching them to observe all things what-soever I have commanded you: and, lo, I am with you always, even unto the end of the world. Amen*
(Matthew 28:19-20).

*And He said unto them, I must preach the kingdom of God to other cities also: for therefore am I sent*
(Luke 4:43).

# PRAYER FOR SIGNIFICANCE

I want approval, acceptance, affirmation, and encouragement. That is not unusual for anyone to desire. My desire, however, has become obsessive, because I seek for significance anywhere and everywhere.

I create situations to get attention. I fake my emotions to get response. I overdo in order to compete or surpass others. I am just out of control. Although I do have reasons for this need, You, Lord, died on the cross to give me a different kind of life. This life is free from bondages.

My quest for importance has become oppressive. I want to find my true self and being in You. I want to be approved and affirmed by You. The world is cruel and insensitive towards who I am and why I am on this earth. You, Lord, made me. You love and sustain me. Help me to be confident in this, at peace with this, and surrounded by this. I praise You for the release from the slavery of praise-seeking into the freedom of praise-giving. Thank You, Lord.

*A man that flattereth his neighbour
spreadeth a net for his feet*
(Proverbs 29:5).

*As the refining pot for silver, and the furnace
for gold; so is a man to his praise*
(Proverbs 27:21).

*For do I now persuade men, or God? or do I
seek to please men? for if I yet pleased men,
I should not be the servant of Christ*
(Galatians 1:10).

*For we are His workmanship, created in Christ
Jesus unto good works, which God hath before
ordained that we should walk in them*
(Ephesians 2:10).

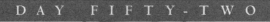

# PRAYER FOR THE HIGH PRAISE

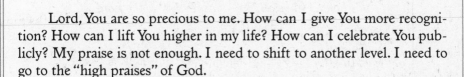

Lord, You are so precious to me. How can I give You more recognition? How can I lift You higher in my life? How can I celebrate You publicly? My praise is not enough. I need to shift to another level. I need to go to the "high praises" of God.

You said in Your Word that this kind of praise is warfare praise. You said that praises touch Your heart and release Your power to intervene on my behalf. I will raise my voice louder; I will declare Your praise fuller; and I will lift my hands higher. I will bless You, adore You, exalt You, and love You. This praise will be a high praise!

*Let the saints be joyful in glory: let them sing aloud upon their beds. Let the high praises of God be in their mouth, and a twoedged sword in their hand; to execute vengeance upon the heathen, and punishments upon the people; to bind their kings with chains, and their nobles with fetters of iron; to execute upon them the judgment written: this honour have all His saints. Praise ye the Lord*
(Psalm 149:5-9).

*And one cried unto another, and said, Holy, holy, holy, is the Lord of hosts: the whole earth is full of His glory*
(Isaiah 6:3).

*Then the spirit took me up, and I heard behind me a voice of a great rushing, saying, Blessed be the glory of the Lord from His place*
(Ezekiel 3:12).

*And after these things I heard a great voice of much people in heaven, saying, Alleluia; Salvation, and glory, and honour, and power, unto the Lord our God*
(Revelation 19:1).

# PRAYER FOR MORE GRACE

Every rung on the ladder of life takes me into a new place of challenge and opportunity. These opportunities afford me the privilege of seeing my inner self. I am forced to face myself, without the mask and from under the covers. I have discovered that I cannot make this journey on my own.

I must implore Your grace, Your favor, Your strength, Your courage, and Your wisdom. These are the virtues that will take me through the day-to-day activity, experience, and encounter of my passage. Intelligence, wit, talent, and connection cannot suffice for this place in my life. Your grace, however, is enough. As a matter a fact, it is more than enough. All I want is more and more of Your grace and Your favor for life. Your favor is better than life. Thank You, Lord!

*For His anger endureth but a moment; in
His favour is life: weeping may endure for a
night, but joy cometh in the morning*
(Psalm 30:5).

*Who art thou, O great mountain? before Zerubbabel thou
shalt become a plain: and he shall bring forth the headstone
thereof with shoutings, crying, Grace, grace unto it*
(Zechariah 4:7).

*And of His fulness have all we received, and
grace for grace. For the law was given by Moses,
but grace and truth came by Jesus Christ*
(John 1:16-17).

*For if by one man's offence death reigned by one; much
more they which receive abundance of grace and of the gift
of righteousness shall reign in life by one, Jesus Christ*
(Romans 5:17).

# PRAYER TO BREAK BARRIERS

Some days I wake up, Lord, and feel as if a tanker has run over me.

Helplessness, hopelessness, and feebleness set in. I want to move, but feel completely immobilized. I sometimes feel that some unseen force is holding me back, stifling me and restricting me.

I know that these barriers are sent to block me from enjoying the precious moments that You have afforded me. These barriers attempt to do what Jericho tried to do to the nation of Israel in Bible times. Israel conquered and uprooted the walls of obstruction; therefore, I can do the same in Your name, Jesus.

I will overcome because of Your intervention and guidance. There is no stumbling block that can prevent me from moving forward. I feel my help already. Thank You for Your divine help, Lord!

*So the people shouted when the priests blew with the trum-*
*pets: and it came to pass, when the people heard the sound of*
*the trumpet, and the people shouted with a great shout, that*
*the wall fell down flat, so that the people went up into the*
*city, every man straight before him, and they took the city*
(Joshua 6:20).

*And David came to Baal-perazim, and David smote*
*them there, and said, The Lord hath broken forth upon*
*mine enemies before me, as the breach of waters. Therefore*
*he called the name of that place Baal-perazim*
(2 Samuel 5:20).

*For by Thee I have run through a troop; and*
*by my God have I leaped over a wall*
(Psalm 18:29).

# PRAYER FOR THE VISION

The word "vision" has been used so loosely that I don't know what to expect when I say it. What I do know, Lord, is that I have bursts of inspiration that bring me closer to You. I catch glimpses of Your thoughts floating through my mind and flashes of Your anointing igniting my spirit. It is these moments that I feel strongly motivated to create or activate these thoughts.

I keep my pencil and paper with me, along with my Bible, and I sketch these ideas randomly until I find a connection. When this connection comes, I begin to see a pattern or a course. This is what I call "vision." I now pray for the grace to keep tuned into You, to keep faithful to the pattern, and to be conscious of the connections. The resources can come only from You, and the reality can be realized only in You. Thank You for vision that comes to pass at the right time.

*And look that thou make them after their*
*pattern, which was shown thee in the mount*
(Exodus 25:40).

*Then David gave to Solomon his son the pattern of*
*the porch, and of the houses thereof, and of the treasuries*
*thereof, and of the upper chambers thereof, and of the*
*inner parlours thereof, and of the place of the mercy seat,*
*and the pattern of all that he had by the spirit, of the*
*courts of the house of the Lord, and of all the chambers*
*round about, of the treasuries of the house of God, and of*
*the treasuries of the dedicated things....All this, said*
*David, the Lord made me understand in writing by His*
*hand upon me, even all the works of this pattern*
(1 Chronicles 28:11-12,19).

*Where there is no vision, the people perish:*
*but he that keepeth the law, happy is he*
(Proverbs 29:18).

# PRAYER AGAINST SELF-LOVE

I am desperately in need of Your deliverance from myself. You said in Your Word that I should love my neighbor as myself, but it must be done in the context of loving You with my whole being. I do love You, Lord, but not like that. I have tried and tried, but I just can't let myself go to the point where You are everything to me. I feel petrified of losing me and never finding me. Most of my life, I have had to protect, defend, and care for myself. I have been neglected and abandoned; therefore, I must take care of me.

This attitude, however, causes me to miss out on the freedom of giving love and receiving love. I am anxious to experience love that brings healing and nurturing. I know that I can't walk in this, if I don't let go of self. Please help me to let self go, so that self can become alive and fulfilled. Please, Father, let this experience open up to me with Your guidance and Your grace. I wait with much expectancy. Bless You, Lord!

*Thou shalt not avenge, nor bear any grudge against
the children of thy people, but thou shalt love thy
neighbour as thyself: I am the Lord*
(Leviticus 19:18).

*For whosoever will save his life shall lose it: but whosoever
will lose his life for My sake, the same shall save it*
(Luke 9:24).

[Charity] *doth not behave itself unseemly, seeketh not
her own, is not easily provoked, thinketh no evil*
(1 Corinthians 13:5).

# PRAYER TO SEE

I am not physically blind, but I live as if I cannot see. My fast-paced life causes me to run hither and thither without looking. Sure, I see the things that I need to see in order to maintain my world. But I am so restricted in my vision that worlds have passed me by; consequently, I have totally missed or ignored them.

You stopped me, Lord, and made me see the physically blind seeing with their ears, exploring with their touch, and envisioning with their smell. When I saw how they reached for life through their limited senses, I became ashamed and convicted.

Please hear my prayer for sight. I want to stop and look at people differently. I want to see the sun go down even on a cloudy night. I want to see the squirrel jumping from limb to limb, the dog standing on his hind legs, and the cat contentedly purring on someone's lap. I have missed smiles, starlights, and autumn hues. I have been blinded by my own tunnel vision. Give sight, Lord, and I will see Your beauty, Your goodness, and Your marvels.

*Then Jesus answering said unto them, Go your way, and tell John what things ye have seen and heard; how that the blind see, the lame walk, the lepers are cleansed, the deaf hear, the dead are raised, to the poor the gospel is preached* (Luke 7:22).

*He answered and said, Whether he be a sinner or no, I know not: one thing I know, that, whereas I was blind, now I see* (John 9:25).

*But he that lacketh these things is blind, and cannot see afar off, and hath forgotten that he was purged from his old sins* (2 Peter 1:9).

# PRAYER AGAINST COMPUTER MISUSE

This is the age of high technology and scientific breakthroughs. The computer has become a necessity and not a luxury. I am amazed that I am computer literate. I can surf the Internet and become a part of anything, anywhere and at any time.

When I log on to the computer, I feel intelligent, resourceful, and uninhibited. I can change my name, my hair, my gender, and my life by tapping a key and clicking a button. What it has done, however, is put me in a zone of fantasy and deception. I have clicked buttons that have connected me to experiences that deceived me and caused me to disrupt my relationship with You, Lord.

This machine can be as seductive as a sensual lover and can be as controlling as an addictive substance. A machine now traps me. I can't wait to get to the computer for the e-mails, the websites, and the games. This activity has sapped my spiritual energy and eclipsed my love for You. Please help me to gain control, because I am out of control. This technology was created to help me reach the world for Jesus Christ, not reach the world to satisfy my flesh. I trust Your grace for this need, Lord. Thank You!

*And whatsoever mine eyes desired I kept not from
them, I withheld not my heart from any joy; for my
heart rejoiced in all my labour: and this was my portion
of all my labour. Then I looked on all the works that
my hands had wrought, and on the labour that I had
laboured to do: and, behold, all was vanity and vexation of spirit, and there was no profit under the sun*
(Ecclesiastes 2:10-11).

*Whether therefore ye eat, or drink,
or whatsoever ye do, do all to the glory of God*
(1 Corinthians 10:31).

*Love not the world, neither the things that are in the
world. If any man love the world, the love of the Father
is not in him. For all that is in the world, the lust of
the flesh, and the lust of the eyes, and the pride of
life, is not of the Father, but is of the world*
(1 John 2:15-16).

# PRAYER FOR
# THE SUPPORT TEAM

Lord, You just brought me through a great storm. Everything familiar seemed to have blown away. My stability was threatened and my lifestyle compromised. What would I do without You, Lord, in times like these?

The people whom You placed in my life were the glue that helped to hold me together. You sent praying, loving, caring, and serving people. They were there for me because You laid me on their hearts. They supported me because You empowered them to give. They stood by me because Your grace enabled them to hang in there. I am so grateful to You and to Your angels of mercy. Bless them, Lord. Keep them and fulfill all their godly desires, in Jesus' name.

*But Moses' hands were heavy; and they took a stone,
and put it under him, and he sat thereon; and Aaron
and Hur stayed up his hands, the one on the one side,
and the other on the other side; and his hands were
steady until the going down of the sun
(Exodus 17:12).*

*And Jonathan said to the young man that bare his armour,
Come, and let us go over unto the garrison of these uncircum-
cised: it may be that the Lord will work for us: for there is
no restraint to the Lord to save by many or by few. And his
armourbearer said unto him, Do all that is in thine heart:
turn thee; behold, I am with thee according to thy heart
(1 Samuel 14:6-7).*

*But Jehoshaphat said, Is there not here a prophet of
the Lord, that we may inquire of the Lord by him? And
one of the king of Israel's servants answered and said,
Here is Elisha the son of Shaphat, which poured water
on the hands of Elijah. And Jehoshaphat said, The word
of the Lord is with him. So the king of Israel and
Jehoshaphat and the king of Edom went down to him
(2 Kings 3:11-12).*

# PRAYER TO STAND STILL

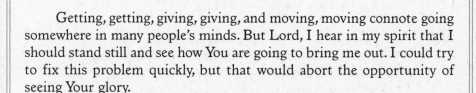

Getting, getting, giving, giving, and moving, moving connote going somewhere in many people's minds. But Lord, I hear in my spirit that I should stand still and see how You are going to bring me out. I could try to fix this problem quickly, but that would abort the opportunity of seeing Your glory.

I must learn to wait for Your glory. Your glory comes when my strength fails. Your glory comes when my solutions peter out. Your glory comes when help from others disappear. I will now stand still and watch Your ingenuity and Your mastery in this situation. Please put a hush in my soul and a calm in my spirit so that I can see Your hand in my life— right now. Thank You, Lord!

*And Moses said unto the people, Fear ye not, stand still, and see the salvation of the Lord, which He will show to you today: for the Egyptians whom ye have seen today, ye shall see them again no more for ever*
(Exodus 14:13).

*He giveth power to the faint; and to them that have no might He increaseth strength. Even the youths shall faint and be weary, and the young men shall utterly fall: but they that wait upon the Lord shall renew their strength; they shall mount up with wings as eagles; they shall run, and not be weary; and they shall walk, and not faint*
(Isaiah 40:29-31).

*And He said unto me, My grace is sufficient for thee: for My strength is made perfect in weakness. Most gladly therefore will I rather glory in my infirmities, that the power of Christ may rest upon me. Therefore I take pleasure in infirmities, in reproaches, in necessities, in persecutions, in distresses for Christ's sake: for when I am weak, then am I strong*
(2 Corinthians 12:9-10).

# PRAYER FROM A TRAVELER

I fly here and there; I drive to and fro; I walk hither and thither; and I sail back and forth experiencing life in many zones. I just want to stop and thank You for Your protection.

You have been my Pilot, my Captain, my Tour Guide, my Caretaker and Protector. I travel for business, pleasure, ministry, and family. Throughout my trafficking, I have had the security of Your arms and Your guidance.

Continue to guide my steps, hold my hands, and keep my heart. Help me to be ever mindful of Your providential care in the sky, on the ground, and on the water. I have this confidence that You will bless my "going out and my coming in" for Your name's sake and for Your glory. Amen, Amen.

*And Abram journeyed, going on still toward the south*
(Genesis 12:9).

*At the commandment of the Lord the children of Israel
journeyed, and at the commandment of the Lord they
pitched: as long as the cloud abode upon the tabernacle
they rested in their tents. And when the cloud tarried
long upon the tabernacle many days, then the children of
Israel kept the charge of the Lord, and journeyed not*
(Numbers 9:18-19).

*And the Lord said unto me, Arise, take thy journey
before the people, that they may go in and possess the
land, which I sware unto their fathers to give unto them*
(Deuteronomy 10:11).

*The Lord shall preserve thy going out and thy coming
in from this time forth, and even for evermore*
(Psalm 121:8).

*Making request, if by any means now at length I might have
a prosperous journey by the will of God to come unto you*
(Romans 1:10).

# PRAYER AND MEDITATION

I read an article recently about meditation, which is becoming more appealing as a secular exercise. Americans are seeking peace, higher spiritual consciousness, and qualifying personal relationships.

As a Christian, I pray, but church life, home life, and everyday life can keep me so busy that I miss quietness and introspection. I have been taught to pray, worship, praise, and fellowship; but I have never been taught to sit still and meditate.

I need to find a place where I stop and think on Your goodness, Your faithfulness, Your kindness, Your wisdom, and Your truth. I need to relax in the warmth of Your arms and draw from the tenderness of Your heart.

Teach me to drink from Your fountain quietly and gaze into Your presence freely. Please let me come away with You into that place of solitude, without fear of stillness, loneliness, or alienation.

In Your presence there is comfort; under the shadow of Your wings is divine protection; and in Your Word is strength and power. Thank You, Lord, for the awareness to stop and think about You.

*This book of the law shall not depart out of thy
mouth; but thou shalt meditate therein day and night,
that thou mayest observe to do according to all that is
written therein: for then thou shalt make thy way
prosperous, and then thou shalt have good success
(Joshua 1:8).*

*Thou wilt keep him in perfect peace, whose mind is
stayed on Thee: because he trusteth in Thee
(Isaiah 26:3).*

*I was in the Spirit on the Lord's day, and heard
behind me a great voice, as of a trumpet
(Revelation 1:10).*

*And it came to pass, that, when I was
come again to Jerusalem, even while I prayed
in the temple, I was in a trance
(Acts 22:17).*

# PRAYER FROM A FATHER AND SON

FATHER: This boy is mine, the gift that You gave us. We are still trying to fathom Your creativity in the conception and birth of our son. I played with nieces and nephews for years, but holding and playing with my son is different.

SON: Lord, it has been 20 years since my birth, but my dad still hugs and looks at me as if I am a newborn baby. He cries when I hug him and sticks his chest out when I share my dreams. I have watched him age with the glory of being a sage. The lines and wrinkles of time dress his skin, but the warmth of his love is stronger within.

FATHER: The greatest gift of all is that my son accepted You as his personal Savior. He strayed away during his teen years, but on his 19th birthday, he answered the call. I have been praising You since that day. You have kept him, guided him, and chastened him.

SON: Lord, please give us some more years together. I need the security of his love and commitment. I need to give him my love and fidelity, because that's what a son can do.

FATHER & SON: Thank You, Lord. You are the only One who can take this relationship from biology into spirituality.

*And give unto Solomon my son a perfect heart, to keep Thy commandments, Thy testimonies, and Thy statutes, and to do all these things, and to build the palace, for the which I have made provision* (1 Chronicles 29:19).

*Children's children are the crown of old men; and the glory of children are their fathers* (Proverbs 17:6).

*And He shall go before Him in the spirit and power of Elias, to turn the hearts of the fathers to the children, and the disobedient to the wisdom of the just; to make ready a people prepared for the Lord* (Luke 1:17).

# Prayer for Sowing and Reaping

Giving of my time, love, talent, and resources can be very exhausting. I am challenged by waiting for the reaping. This waiting period forces me to deal with fear, apprehension, and doubt. I have the Word of the Lord that says that after sowing comes reaping.

The unending question during the period of waiting is: "How long, Lord, how long?" The more I ask this question, the longer it seems I have to wait. During this time, I often become depressed, because I feel that I am wasting my time and missing the mark.

I obey You as much as I can, yet I feel that others who do not obey have it so much easier. They seem to prosper. I get so consumed, at times, with their so-called "prosperity" that I forget to count my blessings.

I want to experience my days with You, Lord, differently. Please help me overcome every feeling of doubt and fear. Also, help me rise above my hopelessness, seeing strength in defeat and glory in despair. I cannot do this through intellectual language and thoughts, nor with cosmetic makeovers and fashion statements. This must be done by Your divine intervention. I am open and desperately in need of Your healing power and Your balmy wind of cheer. Thank You, Lord, in advance!

*While the earth remaineth, seedtime and harvest,*
*and cold and heat, and summer and winter,*
*and day and night shall not cease*
(Genesis 8:22).

*Turn again our captivity, O Lord, as the streams in the*
*south. They that sow in tears shall reap in joy. He that*
*goeth forth and weepeth, bearing precious seed, shall doubt-*
*less come again with rejoicing, bringing his sheaves with him*
(Psalm 126:4-6).

*Be not deceived; God is not mocked: for whatsoever a*
*man soweth, that shall he also reap. For he that soweth*
*to his flesh shall of the flesh reap corruption; but he*
*that soweth to the Spirit shall of the Spirit reap life*
*everlasting. And let us not be weary in well doing:*
*for in due season we shall reap, if we faint not*
(Galatians 6:7-9).

# PRAYER AGAINST THE FEAR OF EVIL

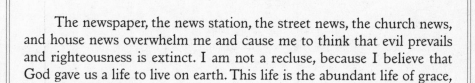

The newspaper, the news station, the street news, the church news, and house news overwhelm me and cause me to think that evil prevails and righteousness is extinct. I am not a recluse, because I believe that God gave us a life to live on earth. This life is the abundant life of grace, truth, joy, and peace.

However, sin, injustice, rebellion, ungodliness, and the like reign and reek in the fiber of our society. I do pray, Lord, that Your grace covers, protects, and overcomes the power of evil thoughts, evil actions, and evil words.

Evil comes dressed up in the garment of power, clod in the glory of deception, and donned in the costume of pleasure. This fun-loving, self-indulging, and super-thrilling lifestyle promises a quality of life that is very seductive and enticing to the superficial eye. Underneath, it delivers far less than what it promises.

Lord, help the Church to bring ourselves under, so that we will not be drawn away by our own lust. Teach us how to get over the moment and reach for the next hour of victory and freedom. This freedom will render us incapable of succumbing to the power of our appetites. We will not become slaves to destructive energies and influences. Thank You, Lord.

*Shall the throne of iniquity have fellowship with Thee, which frameth mischief by a law? They gather themselves together against the soul of the righteous, and condemn the innocent blood. But the Lord is my defence; and my God is the rock of my refuge*
(Psalm 94:20-22).

*It is time for Thee, Lord, to work: for they have made void Thy law*
(Psalm 119:126).

*And moreover I saw under the sun the place of judgment, that wickedness was there; and the place of righteousness, that iniquity was there*
(Ecclesiastes 3:16).

*The just Lord is in the midst thereof; He will not do iniquity: every morning doth He bring His judgment to light, He faileth not; but the unjust knoweth no shame*
(Zephaniah 3:5).

*Nevertheless the foundation of God standeth sure, having this seal, The Lord knoweth them that are His. And, Let every one that nameth the name of Christ depart from iniquity*
(2 Timothy 2:19).

# PRAYER TO GET PAST THE ROUGH MOMENT

There are times when a moment can seem like a century. These moments are usually full of stress and uncertainty. It is amazing how time seems to stand still when pain is being experienced. These moments attract the spirit of the enemy of our souls, who maximizes our sorrow and shrouds our joy.

Lord, let Your Word lift me and carry me out of this moment unscathed. There is so much that I can learn about myself in this tunnel of darkness. How I see, hear, feel, decide, react, and think, direct and compel my steps through the valley of ambiguity.

I know that "weeping may endure for a night, but joy cometh in the morning" (Ps. 30:5) is one of Your promises to the believing heart. It just seems so far away during the dark moments. I rise, however, in Your Spirit, in the name of Jesus. I pant with words of hope on my lips, in the name of Jesus. I lie in Your arms of strength and comfort, in the name of Jesus. I know that I will triumph in Your name, Jesus.

*Yea, though I walk through the valley of the
shadow of death, I will fear no evil: for Thou art
with me; Thy rod and Thy staff they comfort me*
(Psalm 23:4).

*I had fainted, unless I had believed to see the
goodness of the Lord in the land of the living. Wait
on the Lord: be of good courage, and He shall
strengthen thine heart: wait, I say, on the Lord*
(Psalm 27:13-14).

*For I reckon that the sufferings of this present
time are not worthy to be compared with the
glory which shall be revealed in us*
(Romans 8:18).

*For which cause we faint not; but though our outward
man perish, yet the inward man is renewed day by day.
For our light affliction, which is but for a moment, worketh
for us a far more exceeding and eternal weight of glory;
while we look not at the things which are seen, but at the
things which are not seen: for the things which are seen are
temporal; but the things which are not seen are eternal*
(2 Corinthians 4:16-18).

# PRAYER OF TRANSFORMATION

So many things have happened in the past years and months that I just can't keep up with the changes. The rapidity and consistency of my transformation have thrust me into a new attitude of praise and worship.

I am so inundated with wonder that words fail to express what I feel. I sense my passions moving into a healthy and positive vein. I stand outside of myself and watch myself overcome my anger and fear. I see my spirit rise and become free in the intimacy of Your presence, Lord. I am no longer intimidated by the notion of waiting, but find creative ways of passing the time. Transformation is truly visible. *Thank You, Lord!*

*And be not conformed to this world: but be ye transformed by the renewing of your mind, that ye may prove what is that good, and acceptable, and perfect, will of God* (Romans 12:2).

*But we all, with open face beholding as in a glass the glory of the Lord, are changed into the same image from glory to glory, even as by the Spirit of the Lord* (2 Corinthians 3:18).

*And beside this, giving all diligence, add to your faith virtue; and to virtue knowledge; and to knowledge temperance; and to temperance patience; and to patience godliness; and to godliness brotherly kindness; and to brotherly kindness charity. For if these things be in you, and abound, they make you that ye shall neither be barren nor unfruitful in the knowledge of our Lord Jesus Christ* (2 Peter 1:5-8).

# PRAYER FOR A FAST

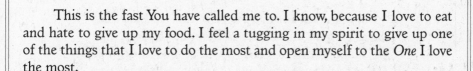

This is the fast You have called me to. I know, because I love to eat and hate to give up my food. I feel a tugging in my spirit to give up one of the things that I love to do the most and open myself to the *One* I love the most.

Food soothes me, excites me, and sates me temporarily. I hunger, however, for righteousness and holiness. I need more of You and want less of me. There is no struggle in my heart for this closer walk with You, Lord. I just ask You for grace to deny myself of the pleasure of food and seek the pleasure of Your company and Your intimacy. Please change my taste buds so that I can sustain the abstinence from food for this momentary journey.

You said in Your Word that fasting affords us greater access to Your power and authority. I need to feel confident in my place and position in the Kingdom. This fast will release me to walk with that authority. I rebuke headaches, nausea, stomach cramps, dizziness, lethargy, and irritability. Help me to prepare adequately for the fast so that my physical needs will not distract me from achieving my spiritual desires. Flood me with peace and solace. Grant my petitions according to Your will and purpose. Bless You, Lord!

*Neither have I gone back from the commandment of His lips; I have esteemed the words of His mouth more than my necessary food*
(Job 23:12).

*Is not this the fast that I have chosen? to loose the bands of wickedness, to undo the heavy burdens, and to let the oppressed go free, and that ye break every yoke? Is it not to deal thy bread to the hungry, and that thou bring the poor that are cast out to thy house? when thou seest the naked, that thou cover him; and that thou hide not thyself from thine own flesh?*
(Isaiah 58:6-7)

*And I set my face unto the Lord God, to seek by prayer and supplications, with fasting, and sackcloth, and ashes*
(Daniel 9:3).

*Howbeit this kind goeth not out but by prayer and fasting*
(Matthew 17:21).

# PRAYER FROM A MOTHER AND DAUGHTER

MOTHER: Dear Lord, I have tried to have a good relationship with my daughter, but she seems so far away from my touch. This cannot be the little girl whose hair I curled, whose dresses I ironed, and whose nose I cleaned. She is independent, yet appears to be so needy. We just can't communicate. Help me to touch her with Your touch and with Your wisdom.

DAUGHTER: I want my mother to be proud of me, but I am experiencing and doing things that I am not proud of. I feel myself slipping away from my family's values, but I just can't stop myself right now. I wish I could tell Mom without being judged. I wish I could put my head in her lap and ask her to kiss my troubles away. I fear her disapproval and rejection. Please help me, Lord!

MOTHER: Lord, she does not know that I was in her shoes years before. She also does not know that I am aware of her activities and her downfalls. I have to deal with my anger and frustration before I reach out to her. I don't want to drive her away, yet I am not in agreement with her lifestyle. How do I reach her, Lord?

MOTHER & DAUGHTER: We need time, Lord—time to forgive each other and time to heal each other. Give us a chance to walk through this season without condemnation or judgment. This relationship is worth saving; therefore, give us knowledge and understanding. We trust Your guidance, Jesus.

*Honour thy father and thy mother, as the Lord thy
God hath commanded thee; that thy days may be
prolonged, and that it may go well with thee, in
the land which the Lord thy God giveth thee*
(Deuteronomy 5:16).

*That our sons may be as plants grown up in their
youth; that our daughters may be as corner
stones, polished after the similitude of a palace*
(Psalm 144:12).

*And it shall come to pass afterward, that I will pour
out My spirit upon all flesh; and your sons and your
daughters shall prophesy, your old men shall dream
dreams, your young men shall see visions*
(Joel 2:28).

*When I call to remembrance the unfeigned faith that is in
thee, which dwelt first in thy grandmother Lois, and thy
mother Eunice; and I am persuaded that in thee also*
(2 Timothy 1:5).

# PRAYER FOR THE LONG DISTANCE

They are there, and I am here. The distance is wearing me out, Lord. My telephone bills are high and my days for travel are gone. I sense trouble around them, but I am too far to help them. How do I rest in spite of the distance? How do I pray when they are so far away?

I read in Your Word that You sent the Word to the centurion's home and his servant was healed. Send Your Word of healing, deliverance, and prosperity to my loved ones. Please remember their needs and intervene on their behalf. I can't go, but Your Word can travel and accomplish what You sent it to do. Speak it, Lord, and it will reach the four corners of the world. I believe and have faith in the power of Your spoken Word. Amen!

*He sent His word, and healed them, and*
*delivered them from their destructions*
(Psalm 107:20).

*He sendeth forth His commandment upon*
*earth: His word runneth very swiftly*
(Psalm 147:15).

*So shall My word be that goeth forth out of My*
*mouth: it shall not return unto Me void, but it*
*shall accomplish that which I please, and it shall*
*prosper in the thing whereto I sent it*
(Isaiah 55:11).

*And Jesus said unto the centurion, Go thy way;*
*and as thou hast believed, so be it done unto thee.*
*And his servant was healed in the selfsame hour*
(Matthew 8:13).

# PRAYER FOR STEWARDSHIP

Generous and bountiful describe Your providential care for me. You have created me with so much life, endowment, and ability. Because You are the Creator, I have a piece of Your power within me. I, however, have neglected to embrace these gifts, cultivate these potentials, and release these talents.

Fear, insecurity, selfishness, rebellion, and ignorance are enemies of the true me. I now see it, and I need Your help to face the worst of me in You so that I can become the best of me through You. Oh Lord, I await this disclosure, and I vow to flow with the discoveries, under Your divine guidance. Thank You, Lord!

*So God created man in His own image, in the image
of God created He him; male and female created He
them. And God blessed them, and God said unto
them, Be fruitful, and multiply, and replenish the
earth, and subdue it: and have dominion over the
fish of the sea, and over the fowl of the air, and over
every living thing that moveth upon the earth*
(Genesis 1:27-28).

*I wisdom dwell with prudence,
and find out knowledge of witty inventions*
(Proverbs 8:12).

*And unto one he gave five talents, to another two,
and to another one; to every man according to his
several ability; and straightway took his journey. Then
he that had received the five talents went and traded
with the same, and made them other five talents*
(Matthew 25:15-16).

*Moreover it is required in stewards,
that a man be found faithful*
(1 Corinthians 4:2).

*As every man hath received the gift, even
so minister the same one to another, as good
stewards of the manifold grace of God*
(1 Peter 4:10).

# PRAYER FOR MERCY

Lord, daily I receive mercy from Your hand. There isn't a day when I do not see and experience Your goodness. I am the beneficiary of Your compassion, not Your wrath and rejection.

I have done what I wanted to do for most of my life. Now I am ready to apply Your forgiveness, dwell under Your shadow, and snuggle up into Your grace. Mercy, Lord!

*With the merciful Thou wilt show Thyself merciful, and
with the upright man Thou wilt show Thyself upright*
(2 Samuel 22:26).

*Mercy and truth are met together;
righteousness and peace have kissed each other*
(Psalm 85:10).

*He that followeth after righteousness and
mercy findeth life, righteousness, and honour*
(Proverbs 21:21).

*He hath shown thee, O man, what is good; and what
doth the Lord require of thee, but to do justly, and to
love mercy, and to walk humbly with thy God?*
(Micah 6:8)

*Blessed are the merciful: for they shall obtain mercy*
(Matthew 5:7).

# PRAYER AGAINST LAZINESS

The Bible calls laziness "sluggishness," which means "slothfulness." I admit that there is a spirit that pulls me into a state of rebellion, absentmindedness, neglect, and avoidance.

If I can get around it, get by it, or get past it, then I will not do it. I will leave it for someone else to do for me. This is a reflection of how I was raised as a child. I have never been challenged to be industrious as the ant, mentioned in the Book of Proverbs. Consequently, I have rarely excelled economically, spiritually, and socially. I surrender that spirit of slothfulness. Now, Lord, I thank You for the burst of energy and the quest for life.

Prayer for my waterless trees, flowers, plants, and fruits will reflect Your glory and beauty. Many sermons are preached about fruitlessness and uselessness, but they never moved me until now. I will release my trust in You that You will charge me and ignite fresh fire in me to do and to become all that pleases You. Amen!

*Go to the ant, thou sluggard; consider her ways, and be wise:*
*which having no guide, overseer, or ruler, provideth her meat*
*in the summer, and gathereth her food in the harvest*
(Proverbs 6:6-8).

*The soul of the sluggard desireth, and hath nothing:*
*but the soul of the diligent shall be made fat*
(Proverbs 13:4).

*And when He saw a fig tree in the way, He came to it,*
*and found nothing thereon, but leaves only, and said*
*unto it, Let no fruit grow on thee henceforward for*
*ever. And presently the fig tree withered away*
(Matthew 21:19).

*His lord answered and said unto him, Thou wicked and*
*slothful servant, thou knewest that I reap where I sowed*
*not, and gather where I have not strawed: thou oughtest*
*therefore to have put my money to the exchangers, and then*
*at my coming I should have received mine own with usury*
(Matthew 25:26-27).

*That ye be not slothful, but followers of them who*
*through faith and patience inherit the promises*
(Hebrews 6:12).

# PRAYER FOR PROPERTY

This is a miracle, Lord—for me and my family! It is not a miracle for You, because "the earth is Yours and the fullness thereof" (Ps. 24:1a). I have never owned land; my family has never owned a house; and my parents have never bought property. This is my first home, and it happened in spite of my meager finances.

Please give me the commitment to be a good steward over this place. Help me to open my doors to the stranger and to always give You thanks for this place. This is more than a sleeping place, but a talking place, a loving place, and a nurturing place. Thanks for the home that You gave me.

*And the Lord said unto Abram, after that Lot was separated from him, Lift up now thine eyes, and look from the place where thou art northward, and southward, and eastward, and westward: for all the land which thou seest, to thee will I give it, and to thy seed for ever. And I will make thy seed as the dust of the earth: so that if a man can number the dust of the earth, then shall thy seed also be numbered. Arise, walk through the land in the length of it and in the breadth of it; for I will give it unto thee* (Genesis 13:14-17).

*And he removed from thence, and digged another well; and for that they strove not: and he called the name of it Rehoboth; and he said, For now the Lord hath made room for us, and we shall be fruitful in the land* (Genesis 26:22).

*She considereth a field, and buyeth it: with the fruit of her hands she planteth a vineyard....She looketh well to the ways of her household, and eateth not the bread of idleness* (Proverbs 31:16,27).

# Prayer From the Wealthy

Lord, You have blessed me abundantly. You have granted cash and property into my hands and my life. I have received from You what people dream of in their lifetime. Everything that I put my hands to, You have multiplied and increased.

I wish I had thousands of tongues to thank You minute by minute. I know that it is easy to forget to pray, when I have the funds to play. I know I can ignore You because I have the means to do my own thing. I know I can become greedy, because I don't have many reasons to heed.

But, oh God, I need Your wisdom in order to experience heavenly wealth.

*But thou shalt remember the Lord thy God: for it is He that giveth thee power to get wealth, that He may establish His covenant which he sware unto thy fathers, as it is this day* (Deuteronomy 8:18).

*Lay not up for yourselves treasures upon earth, where moth and rust doth corrupt, and where thieves break through and steal: but lay up for yourselves treasures in heaven, where neither moth nor rust doth corrupt, and where thieves do not break through nor steal: for where your treasure is, there will your heart be also* (Matthew 6:19-21).

*For the love of money is the root of all evil: which while some coveted after, they have erred from the faith, and pierced themselves through with many sorrows....Charge them that are rich in this world, that they be not high-minded, nor trust in uncertain riches, but in the living God, who giveth us richly all things to enjoy* (1 Timothy 6:10,17).

# PRAYER FOR FULL JOY

Walking with You, Lord, can be so challenging that there is no delight or jubilance in my relationship with You. The continual attacks and counterattacks drain and deplete my energy level.

There are so many waves of depression and frustration that overflow my spirit and attempt to drown my soul. I do love You, Lord, but when I feel so helpless, I cannot raise my hand high and open my lips wide to praise You.

I am sure that You see my vulnerability and know my weaknesses. Please have mercy on me and restore to me the joy of my salvation. I need to be refreshed, renewed, and rejuvenated. I want my joy back, which strengthens me in weary times. I will praise You until I sense the depths of Your love and care for me, which will release Your joy in me.

*Then he said unto them, Go your way, eat the fat, and
drink the sweet, and send portions unto them for whom
nothing is prepared: for this day is holy unto our Lord:
neither be ye sorry; for the joy of the Lord is your strength*
(Nehemiah 8:10).

*Thou wilt show me the path of life: in Thy presence is fulness
of joy; at Thy right hand there are pleasures for evermore*
(Psalm 16:11).

*His lord said unto him, Well done, thou good and
faithful servant: thou hast been faithful over a
few things, I will make thee ruler over many
things: enter thou into the joy of thy lord*
(Matthew 25:21).

*For the kingdom of God is not meat and drink;
but righteousness, and peace, and joy in the Holy Ghost*
(Romans 14:17).

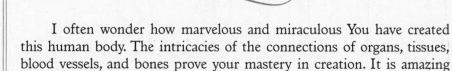

# PRAYER FOR THE STRENGTHENING OF MY HEART

I often wonder how marvelous and miraculous You have created this human body. The intricacies of the connections of organs, tissues, blood vessels, and bones prove your mastery in creation. It is amazing how the human heart pumps and sustains every movement, activity, and function of my body.

With this in mind, I can come to You, the Maker of my heart, for healing and wholeness of my inner self. When my heart is weak and fragile, I feel helpless, motionless, and restless. When my heart is broken, I feel lost, unwanted, and misdirected. My prayer is: Please strengthen the fiber of my wounded, tired, and feeble heart.

I have a great journey ahead of me and I need to be strengthened and energized to travel on. I feel so alive, when my heart is strong. I feel so motivated, when my heart is whole. I feel so healthy, when my heart is cleansed. Heal me and I shall be healed, Lord. Strengthen my heart and I shall be complete, Lord. Amen!

*And the Lord thy God will circumcise thine heart, and the heart of thy seed, to love the Lord thy God with all thine heart, and with all thy soul, that thou mayest live*
(Deuteronomy 30:6).

*Wait on the Lord: be of good courage, and He shall strengthen thine heart: wait, I say, on the Lord*
(Psalm 27:14).

*Create in me a clean heart, O God; and renew a right spirit within me*
(Psalm 51:10).

*Truly God is good to Israel, even to such as are of a clean heart*
(Psalm 73:1).

*To the end He may stablish your hearts unblameable in holiness before God, even our Father, at the coming of our Lord Jesus Christ with all His saints*
(1 Thessalonians 3:13).

# PRAYER FOR A TRUTHFUL TONGUE

Lord, there are those moments when I see and hear things about others, and consequently, I become a witness to the circumstance. I am then placed in a position to speak on behalf of that person's character. The situation, however, may be very sensitive, because I have to put my character and my own self on the line.

I pray that I will not sacrifice truth in order to save myself, my position, or my reputation. This is easier said than done, because the risk factor could be very high. I have watched others twist the truth to save their neck, which, in turn, caused the victim to suffer needlessly. This stand for being a truthful witness requires courage, justice, and righteousness.

I want to be righteous, Lord; I want to be just, Lord; and I want to be a true witness for someone who is being falsely accused. Thank You, Lord!

*Thou shalt not bear false witness against thy neighbour*
(Exodus 20:16).

*A true witness delivereth souls:*
*but a deceitful witness speaketh lies*
(Proverbs 14:25).

*For out of the heart proceed evil thoughts, murders,*
*adulteries, fornications, thefts, false witness, blasphemies*
(Matthew 15:19).

*And unto the angel of the church of the Laodiceans*
*write; These things saith the Amen, the faithful and*
*true witness, the beginning of the creation of God*
(Revelation 3:14).

# PRAYER FOR
# THE RIGHT CHOICES

Is it me? Is it You, Lord? Is it family or friends? These are the questions that bombard my mind and taunt my spirit. I am often thrown into bewilderment when I am faced with choices that are not obviously Your will.

These choices are not evil or sinful, but they are questionable as to whether I should be doing them or not. These moments can be so sensitive and baffling that I have to just sit and wait on Your leading.

Help me to know Your thoughts on these matters, by any means necessary. Help me to discern Your ways so that I can flow in the right direction. Help me not to look on the appearance, but to hear Your voice in the noise.

I trust Your wisdom, Lord.

*And thine ears shall hear a word behind thee,
saying, This is the way, walk ye in it, when ye turn
to the right hand, and when ye turn to the left
(Isaiah 30:21).*

*And the work of righteousness shall be peace; and the
effect of righteousness quietness and assurance for ever
(Isaiah 32:17).*

*Be careful for nothing; but in every thing by prayer
and supplication with thanksgiving let your requests
be made known unto God. And the peace of God,
which passeth all understanding, shall keep your
hearts and minds through Christ Jesus
(Philippians 4:6-7).*

*For this cause we also, since the day we heard it,
do not cease to pray for you, and to desire that
ye might be filled with the knowledge of His will
in all wisdom and spiritual understanding
(Colossians 1:9).*

# PRAYER AGAINST ANXIETY

There are many times that I panic and fall apart when I face challenges. I have done it for so long, because I don't know what else to do. I love You, Lord, but I am out of control when I face unforeseen circumstances.

When I say "panic," I mean breaking out into cold sweats, repeating sighs, calling people frantically, and pacing to and fro. These kinds of response cause me to become bent out of shape physically, emotionally, and spiritually. This is not what You promised in Your Word. The cry of my soul is to be free from anxiety, alarm, and dread.

I need to take my life out of the hands of hysteria or frenzy. I want Your peace and I need Your assurance to overshadow me and hold me even in the midst of despair. Please teach me how to regain my spirit and bring it into alignment with Your Word and Your Spirit. Thank You, Lord, for the deliverance from this stronghold of anxiety.

*It is in vain that you rise up early and go late to rest, eating the bread of anxious toil; for He gives to His beloved sleep* (Psalm 127:2 ESV).

*Say to those who have an anxious heart, "Be strong; fear not! Behold, your God will come with vengeance, with the recompense of God. He will come and save you"* (Isaiah 35:4 ESV).

*Do not be anxious about anything, but in everything by prayer and supplication with thanksgiving let your requests be made known to God* (Philippians 4:6 ESV).

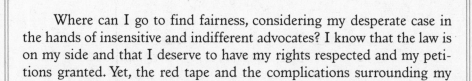

# PRAYER FOR JUSTICE

Where can I go to find fairness, considering my desperate case in the hands of insensitive and indifferent advocates? I know that the law is on my side and that I deserve to have my rights respected and my petitions granted. Yet, the red tape and the complications surrounding my opportunity to receive justice have been extensive.

Lord, hear my plea and grant me favor in this unfavorable situation. I am sure that You will send help, because You are a present help in times of trouble. I anticipate Your divine intervention, Your justice, and Your deliverance. Thank You, Lord.

*Keep thee far from a false matter; and the innocent and righteous slay thou not: for I will not justify the wicked. And thou shalt take no gift: for the gift blindeth the wise, and perverteth the words of the righteous*
(Exodus 23:7-8).

*How long will ye judge unjustly, and accept the persons of the wicked? Selah. Defend the poor and fatherless: do justice to the afflicted and needy. Deliver the poor and needy: rid them out of the hand of the wicked*
(Psalm 82:2-4).

*He that justifieth the wicked, and he that condemneth the just, even they both are abomination to the Lord*
(Proverbs 17:15).

*And shall not God avenge His own elect, which cry day and night unto Him, though He bear long with them? I tell you that He will avenge them speedily. Nevertheless when the Son of man cometh, shall He find faith on the earth?*
(Luke 18:7-8)

# PRAYER FOR REVIVAL

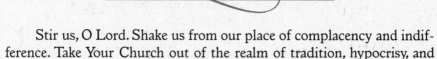

Stir us, O Lord. Shake us from our place of complacency and indifference. Take Your Church out of the realm of tradition, hypocrisy, and folly. Please work in us individually and collectively. We need You to work in us so that our relationship with You takes on meaning and fulfillment.

Pour out Your Spirit in us and through us. Spread Your love and kindness through our speech, action, and expression. Move with Your power, fill us with Your might, and charge us with Your anointing. Revive our hearts and our consciences with Your purpose and will, so that we can represent You and Your Kingdom on earth. Hear us, we pray, O Lord.

*If My people, which are called by My name, shall*
*humble themselves, and pray, and seek My face, and turn*
*from their wicked ways; then will I hear from heaven, and*
*will forgive their sin, and will heal their land*
(2 Chronicles 7:14).

*Wilt Thou not revive us again:*
*that Thy people may rejoice in Thee?*
(Psalm 85:6)

*They that dwell under His shadow shall return; they*
*shall revive as the corn, and grow as the vine: the*
*scent thereof shall be as the wine of Lebanon*
(Hosea 14:7).

*O Lord, I have heard Thy speech, and was afraid:*
*O Lord, revive Thy work in the midst of the years, in the*
*midst of the years make known; in wrath remember mercy*
(Habakkuk 3:2).

# PRAYER AGAINST TEMPTATION

Food everywhere, sex any-and-everywhere, and ego in the air. How am I to resist these luring temptations and live a godly, sober, fulfilled life with moderation?

I don't have to go far, search hard, or look long to find immediate gratification, appeasement, comfort, and satisfaction for my flesh and carnal desires.

My sisters and brothers think that illicit sex is a vice. But gossip, lying, disloyalty, and talebearing are also carnal. It is so easy to embrace these practices, because they can become so irresistible.

Help me, Lord! I believe that nothing should rule me or control me, especially at the expense of my relationship with You, Lord. Please let me look at the prize, which is a life of peace, fulfillment, contentment, and completeness in Your love and care. I probably will not say these words to You when I am overtaken with my passion for self-gratification. I am saying them now, however, so that these words will prevail for me in my moment of weakness.

Give me the grace to stay focused and find the joy in Your wisdom and purpose for my life. Amen.

*And it came to pass, as she spake to Joseph day by day, that*
*he hearkened not unto her, to lie by her, or to be with her*
(Genesis 39:10).

*I have refrained my feet from every*
*evil way, that I might keep Thy word*
(Psalm 119:101).

*And lead us not into temptation, but deliver*
*us from evil: For thine is the kingdom, and*
*the power, and the glory, for ever. Amen*
(Matthew 6:13).

*Watch and pray, that ye enter not into temptation:*
*the spirit indeed is willing, but the flesh is weak*
(Matthew 26:41).

*There hath no temptation taken you but such as is common*
*to man: but God is faithful, who will not suffer you to be*
*tempted above that ye are able; but will with the temptation*
*also make a way to escape, that ye may be able to bear it*
(1 Corinthians 10:13).

# PRAYER FROM A SOLDIER'S HEART

Remember my fellow soldiers, women and men, in a combatant arena, hoping to survive and come out alive. Our prayer and hope is to return home unscathed and alive. We are stationed in a different climate, eating unfamiliar foods, hearing strange languages, and living challenged lives.

Lord, cover our minds, emotions, and spirits! Give us the grace to make the adjustment to fit in our community when we return. It will be different when we get back home, because we are different. Whether we are on the front lines or in a back-up position, we will never be the same.

Let the return be smooth, timely, and wholesome. Let the transition from wartime to peacetime be truly peaceful and therapeutic. We want our lives to move on from this experience without bitterness, hate, or frustration. Remember our loved ones. Give them the grace also to walk through this restoration holding Your hand and connecting it to our hearts.

Thank You, Lord, for this answered prayer.

*Put on the whole armour of God, that ye may be able
to stand against the wiles of the devil. For we wrestle
not against flesh and blood, but against principalities,
against powers, against the rulers of the darkness of
this world, against spiritual wickedness in high places.
Wherefore take unto you the whole armour of God, that
ye may be able to withstand in the evil day, and having
done all, to stand. Stand therefore, having your loins
girt about with truth, and having on the breastplate of
righteousness; and your feet shod with the preparation of
the gospel of peace; above all, taking the shield of faith,
wherewith ye shall be able to quench all the fiery darts
of the wicked. And take the helmet of salvation, and
the sword of the Spirit, which is the word of God*
(Ephesians 6:11-17).

*Thou therefore endure hardness,
as a good soldier of Jesus Christ*
(2 Timothy 2:3).

*But let us, who are of the day, be sober,
putting on the breastplate of faith and love;
and for an helmet, the hope of salvation*
(1 Thessalonians 5:8).

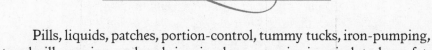

# PRAYER CONCERNING WEIGHT LOSS

Pills, liquids, patches, portion-control, tummy tucks, iron-pumping, treadmill-running, and park-jogging have one aim in mind: to burn fat. The problem is, Lord, the more I do all these things, the more I seem to weigh and look the same.

This weight has aged me, oppressed me, and depreciated me. People have made their sarcastic and cynical remarks, which have driven me further into my fat despair. The thought that losing weight will make me a more attractive, powerful, and confident person prevails throughout my quest for weight loss. I am obsessed, but defeated. My spirit is willing, but my cravings are overwhelming.

Dear Lord, I have discovered that my peace is with You. My acceptance of Your love for me is more important than dieting. It is the discovery of my pain, my disappointment, and my negativism that fosters my cravings for certain kinds of food and a certain time for these foods. The stresses of life and the challenges of my faith cause me to find comfort, at times, in food.

I hear You calling me away from experimenting with crash diets. I, therefore, heed the call to launch out into the deep of relationship with You, Lord, and to trust, even for weight loss. My praise, worship, and discipleship afford me the liberty to release the pain and anxiety of life.

It is this place of relief that gives me the willpower to take charge of my life and find the godly and effective way to bring my temple into the conformity of God's creative purpose. I am no longer possessed or obsessed by the thought of weight loss. I am anointed and empowered to take charge of my life. Lord, please give me the grace to continue on this glorious path.

*I will praise Thee; for I am fearfully and*
*wonderfully made: marvellous are Thy works;*
*and that my soul knoweth right well*
(Psalm 139:14).

*Know ye not that ye are the temple of God,*
*and that the Spirit of God dwelleth in you?*
(1 Corinithians 3:16)

*What? know ye not that your body is the temple*
*of the Holy Ghost which is in you, which*
*ye have of God, and ye are not your own?*
(1 Corinthians 6:19)

*I can do all things through Christ which strengtheneth me*
(Philippians 4:13).

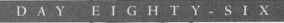

# PRAYER FOR THE SEARCH

Dear Lord, finding answers is not always easy. I love, I serve, I pray to You; but sometimes I can't find You. I know that You are a Spirit, which means that You have no hands or feet. Yet, I can sense Your presence in my heart, in my spirit, in my home, and in the church. Trials come and trials go; nevertheless, I bear them because I can feel Your nearness.

The insufferable moments are the ones when I can't feel You, sense You, or touch You. It is the searching for You, the hoping for You, and the crying out for You that brings me into this panting prayer. Where are You, Lord? Show me Your face! Give me a sign! Make Your way plain! This is my desperate request.

I am searching for You because I refuse to make a decision without Your direction. I reject all of my impulses to dive into any plan or to conceive any agenda without Your approval and Your grace. I will fast and pray. I will sing and praise. I will read and meditate until I hear from You. Your words are more precious to me than diamonds and gold. Sweep over my soul and blow into my anxious heart with Your life and Your Spirit.

Thank You, Lord, for disclosing Yourself so that I can reach You and experience You!

*O God, Thou art my God; early will I seek Thee:*
*my soul thirsteth for Thee, my flesh longeth for*
*Thee in a dry and thirsty land, where no water is*
(Psalm 63:1).

*Ask, and it shall be given you; seek, and ye*
*shall find; knock, and it shall be opened unto you*
(Matthew 7:7).

*That they should seek the Lord, if haply they*
*might feel after Him, and find Him, though*
*He be not far from every one of us*
(Acts 17:27).

*To them who by patient continuance in well doing seek for*
*glory and honour and immortality, eternal life*
(Romans 2:7).

# PRAYER FOR COURAGE

There are some decisions that I find very easy to make, but there are others that render me helpless. When I am faced with these demanding choices, I sometimes freeze or escape.

I try to sleep it away, read it away, talk it away, or ignore it away. The truth is that I become petrified, frustrated, and immobilized at the very thought of choosing "yea" or "nay."

The Word of God does kick in, but when it is a choice in one of the vulnerable areas of my life, I tend to panic. I ask for courage to overcome the immobility. I ask that You breathe Your life into my psyche, and I will rise with courage and grace to tread this thin ice. I am beginning to feel Your strength pulsating in my spiritual veins, as I pray this heartfelt prayer.

Thank You, Jesus, for the courage to come through with victory!

*Be strong and of a good courage, fear not, nor be afraid
of them: for the Lord thy God, He it is that doth go
with thee; He will not fail thee, nor forsake thee*
(Deuteronomy 31:6).

*Have not I commanded thee? Be strong and of a good
courage; be not afraid, neither be thou dismayed: for the
Lord thy God is with thee whithersoever thou goest*
(Joshua 1:9).

*Be of good courage, and He shall strengthen
your heart, all ye that hope in the Lord*
(Psalm 31:24).

*The wicked flee when no man pursueth:
but the righteous are bold as a lion*
(Proverbs 28:1).

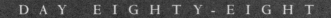

# PRAYER AT THE TURNING POINT

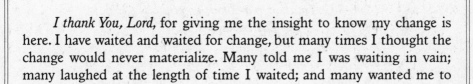

*I thank You, Lord,* for giving me the insight to know my change is here. I have waited and waited for change, but many times I thought the change would never materialize. Many told me I was waiting in vain; many laughed at the length of time I waited; and many wanted me to choose other options.

The options, however, were not to be compared with the glory of Your impending manifestation. It is about to happen, glory to God! I know it in my inner being; I hear with my inner ear and see it with my inner eye.

This great gift of insight impels me to prepare and position myself for the unveiling of Your promise. The heavens are turning, the clouds are bursting, and the waves are gushing under the command of God to deliver my blessing and release my change. I can see it before I can touch it; I can sense it before I can hold it; and I can imagine it before I can appropriate it. Glory to glory, glory to God!

*...all the days of my appointed time*
*will I wait, till my change come*
(Job 14:14).

*But as it is written, Eye hath not seen, nor ear heard,*
*neither have entered into the heart of man, the things*
*which God hath prepared for them that love Him*
(1 Corinthians 2:9).

*While we look not at the things which are seen, but at the*
*things which are not seen: for the things which are seen are*
*temporal; but the things which are not seen are eternal*
(2 Corinthians 4:18).

*Now faith is the substance of things hoped*
*for, the evidence of things not seen*
(Hebrews 11:1).

# PRAYER FOR RESTORATION

Lord, who said it is easy to come back? Who said you can go far out in the world and then come back at any time? Those are irresponsible comments. I went too far, too long, and too deep into worldly pleasure and sinful exploits.

These experiences took me so far from Your presence that it caused me much fear, pain, and turmoil. Yes, I had short-lived pleasure, sensual delights, and temporary friends. Yet, in the midst of it all, I always remembered Your love, Lord. I couldn't shake the memory of Your truth. I couldn't ignore Your steadfast mercy. I wanted to come back many times, but addiction, seduction, shame, and guilt restrained me and conquered me.

It took a moment such as this to break the restraining order from hell and give me back my life with You. *I choose You, Lord. I want You, Lord. I need You, Lord!* Words fail to express the redeeming love that embraced me when I responded to Your recall. Praises will never be sufficient to exalt You for Your forgiving power and tender mercy. My lips utter inadequately the gratitude that I owe to You for this chance to live in Your grace again.

I thank You, Lord, for restoration! I thank You, Lord, for rededication!

*O Israel, return unto the Lord thy God; for thou hast fallen by thine iniquity. Take with you words, and turn to the Lord: say unto Him, Take away all iniquity, and receive us graciously: so will we render the calves of our lips. Asshur shall not save us; we will not ride upon horses: neither will we say any more to the work of our hands, Ye are our gods: for in Thee the fatherless findeth mercy. I will heal their backsliding, I will love them freely: for Mine anger is turned away from him*
(Hosea 14:1-4).

*And the son said unto him, Father, I have sinned against heaven, and in thy sight, and am no more worthy to be called thy son. But the father said to his servants, Bring forth the best robe, and put it on him; and put a ring on his hand, and shoes on his feet: and bring hither the fatted calf, and kill it; and let us eat, and be merry: for this my son was dead, and is alive again; he was lost, and is found. And they began to be merry*
(Luke 15:21-24).

*For the Son of man is come to seek and to save that which was lost*
(Luke 19:10).

# PRAYER AGAINST REJECTION

Why don't they like me, Lord? Why am I the only one whom they ignore? Why is my love unrequited? I can look back in my life and recount the many times that I was looked over, passed by, and left behind. It seems as if it is my life's plight to always be in the rear.

I have spent my life blaming parents, family, friends, and even You, God, for all the times that I felt unwanted. This sensation of being abandoned consumes my mind, minimizes my worth, and cripples my efforts. Lord, You remember how many tantrums and outbursts I had in my prayer and in my worship to You.

I felt that You were treating me unfairly. I also felt that You were punishing me for my past wrongdoings. I challenged Your Word; I challenged Your prophecies; and I challenged Your choices. I blamed so many other people for my life's outcome that I was alienated from good friendships. I drove myself into isolation, frustration, and dissatisfaction.

Please, Lord, take me to that place in You where I can be at peace with myself. Rejection may come, but I will have Your grace and acceptance to override it. I want that place, where You can cover me, shield me, insulate me, and comfort me. It is this place in You that affords me the confidence and resilience to brace the negative and offensive encounters in my life. Thank You, Lord, for this new place in You!

*The stone which the builders refused
is become the head stone of the corner*
(Psalm 118:22).

*Wherefore we labour, that, whether present
or absent, we may be accepted of Him*
(2 Corinthians 5:9).

*To the praise of the glory of His grace, wherein
He hath made us accepted in the beloved*
(Ephesians 1:6).

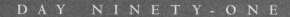

# PRAYER FOR A DISCIPLINED LIFE

"Out of control" best describes my lifestyle. I eat too much, sleep too long, play too hard, gossip too easily, and pray too infrequently. I just want to bring it in, but I lack the strength and stamina. Church is my hangout place, but not my life-changing place.

I want a change, and only You can empower me to embrace that transformation. I know that I have to play a part in this process, but I don't know how to begin. Speak to my will and my heart, and I will open these weak areas to the influence of the Holy Spirit. He is the enabler, He is the motivator, and He is the strong deliverer.

I see order and stability by faith in my daily activity. I see structure with a flow without rigidity. I know my life can be fruitful and productive; therefore, I await the quickening power of Your Spirit to enliven me. It is at this point that You will order my steps by Your Word, Your guidance, and Your arrangement. Lord, hasten the day when I can flow in Your divine order and out from my fleshly disorder. Thank You, Lord.

*He that hath no rule over his own spirit is like a
city that is broken down, and without walls*
(Proverbs 25:28).

*But put ye on the Lord Jesus Christ, and make not
provision for the flesh, to fulfil the lusts thereof*
(Romans 13:14).

*But I keep under my body, and bring it into
subjection: lest that by any means, when I have
preached to others, I myself should be a castaway*
(1 Corinthians 9:27).

# PRAYER FOR
# A.I.D.S. VICTIMS

I see the pain and disappointment in their eyes and wonder how I can bring comfort to this stigmatized and forgotten community. We seldom hear about their struggle unless it is attached to a national crisis. These individuals live with rejection, isolation, emaciation, and deprivation because of this disease and are often neglected and abandoned.

I now stand in the gap for their physical, emotional, and spiritual healing. You are Jehovah Rapha, the Lord that healeth. Reach down, heavenly Father, and release the cure for the physical change; breathe, dear Lord, on their spirits for divine change and comfort them with Your Word for emotional health. I pray with faith, believing that You are able to work a miracle in these people's lives, who are our brothers and sisters. Thank You, Lord, for Your speedy response!

*And said, If thou wilt diligently hearken to the voice of the Lord thy God, and wilt do that which is right in His sight, and wilt give ear to His commandments, and keep all His statutes, I will put none of these diseases upon thee, which I have brought upon the Egyptians: for I am the Lord that healeth thee* (Exodus 15:26).

*But He was wounded for our transgressions, He was bruised for our iniquities: the chastisement of our peace was upon Him; and with His stripes we are healed* (Isaiah 53:5).

*For I will restore health unto thee, and I will heal thee of thy wounds, saith the Lord; because they called thee an Outcast, saying, This is Zion, whom no man seeketh after* (Jeremiah 30:17).

*That it might be fulfilled which was spoken by Esaias the prophet, saying, Himself took our infirmities, and bare our sicknesses* (Matthew 8:17).

*Who His own self bare our sins in His own body on the tree, that we, being dead to sins, should live unto righteousness: by whose stripes ye were healed* (1 Peter 2:24).

# PRAYER TO FILL THE EMPTY SPACES

I am so prone to crowd my space with things, people, and assignments. If my life is not busy, then I feel incomplete and unproductive. There are days when nothing I do seems to satisfy. The assignments that used to consume my energy and give me a thrill, I now find bland and uninviting. What is happening to me, Lord? I ask this question earnestly and continually. Why I am finding boredom in areas where I used to find excitement?

I think I will stop and just take a day and empty my life. I will call it "open space day." This will be the time that I just let it all go for You. I will give You the freedom to write on my pages, to stamp Your print in my spirit, and to etch Your Word in my mind. This is it, Lord. I am a blank sheet of paper ready to be written on. Bless You, Lord!

*Be still, and know that I am God: I will be exalted*
*among the heathen, I will be exalted in the earth*
(Psalm 46:10).

*Better is an handful with quietness, than both the*
*hands full with travail and vexation of spirit*
(Ecclesiastes 4:6).

*For thus saith the Lord God, the Holy One of Israel;*
*In returning and rest shall ye be saved; in quietness*
*and in confidence shall be your strength...*
(Isaiah 30:15).

*And the work of righteousness shall be peace; and the*
*effect of righteousness quietness and assurance for ever*
(Isaiah 32:17).

# PRAYER TO PASS IT ON

A cookbook recipe, a family heirloom, a cultural folklore, or a family album are just some of the things I must pass on. Passing on treasures must become a priority, because the next generation needs this passage to cross over into life. Unfortunately, I am just so busy and caught up into making my own thing come alive that I forget to pass on part of me to the future of me.

Lord, so many of us did not get a "passing on experience." That's why we fail to see the wisdom, the necessity, and the power in giving someone else the chance to start off ahead of the class. Selfishness prevails in my spirit. I wear it, I drink it, and I wallow in it. It is easier to hold to myself, my dreams, my visions and ignore the searching soul who needs a chance to conceptualize a vision.

Lord, grant me the ability to share, to inspire, to motivate, and to kindle the flame of life, of love, of grace, of gift, and of vision. Please challenge me to pass it on. Amen.

*The liberal soul shall be made fat: and he
that watereth shall be watered also himself*
(Proverbs 11:25).

*And if thou draw out thy soul to the hungry, and satisfy
the afflicted soul; then shall thy light rise in obscurity,
and thy darkness be as the noonday: and the Lord shall
guide thee continually, and satisfy thy soul in drought,
and make fat thy bones: and thou shalt be like a watered
garden, and like a spring of water, whose waters fail not*
(Isaiah 58:10-11).

*And this they did, not as we hoped, but first gave their
own selves to the Lord, and unto us by the will of God*
(2 Corinthians 8:5).

# PRAYER FOR THE REVEALING OF SECRETS

Life is full of so many dark places—places that are unfamiliar and unpopular. How do I walk in these places with such little information and limited understanding? I become very angry and irritated because I am not in control. Circumstances will not obey me, life sometimes betrays me, and people often disappoint me.

Dear Lord, open my eyes that I may see Your goodness, Your wisdom, and Your purpose. Move away the fog and clear the mist from my view. Uncover buried secrets, hidden experiences, and masked emotions. I want the truth of Your Word, the truth of Your plan, and the truth of Your will.

This is my daily prayer: Reveal the hidden, and I will walk in the open.

*The secret things belong unto the Lord our God: but those
things which are revealed belong unto us and to our children
for ever, that we may do all the words of this law*
(Deuteronomy 29:29).

*The secret of the Lord is with them that fear Him;
and He will show them His covenant*
(Psalm 25:14).

*Then was the secret revealed unto Daniel in a night
vision. Then Daniel blessed the God of heaven*
(Daniel 2:19).

*Therefore judge nothing before the time, until the Lord
come, who both will bring to light the hidden things of
darkness, and will make manifest the counsels of the
hearts: and then shall every man have praise of God*
(1 Corinthians 4:5).

# PRAYER FOR GODLY FELLOWSHIP

I am a loner, Lord, and find it very difficult to mingle. I have behaved like this from childhood. It is so hard to be a part of a group under any circumstance. I like being alone. I like doing things alone. I love my privacy. The conflict, however, is that I belong to a Christian family, which requires connection, intimacy, fellowship, and relationship. How do I do this, when I am naturally an introvert and emotionally, I am incurably shy?

The discomfort is that even though I want to be alone, I also want to belong and feel a part. I am so discouraged, because I am fearful to take any steps towards meeting and greeting people. I see people doing it and it seems so easy. Help me to find the ease of this. I need to fellowship; I need human contact; and I need to reach out to others. This is what will make my Christian life richer and brighter. This is how I will become complete in You, Lord. This is how human character develops and blossoms. I want to flourish and I want to grow. Thank You, Lord!

*A friend loveth at all times,*
*and a brother is born for adversity*
(Proverbs 17:17).

*A man that hath friends must show himself friendly: and*
*there is a friend that sticketh closer than a brother*
(Proverbs 18:24).

*Iron sharpeneth iron; so a man*
*sharpeneth the countenance of his friend*
(Proverbs 27:17).

*Two are better than one; because they have a good reward*
*for their labour. For if they fall, the one will lift up his*
*fellow: but woe to him that is alone when he falleth; for*
*he hath not another to help him up. Again, if two lie*
*together, then they have heat: but how can one be*
*warm alone? And if one prevail against him, two shall*
*withstand him; and a threefold cord is not quickly broken*
(Ecclesiastes 4:9-12).

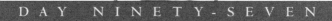

# PRAYER FROM
# AN ADOPTED CHILD

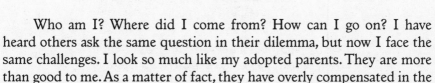

Who am I? Where did I come from? How can I go on? I have heard others ask the same question in their dilemma, but now I face the same challenges. I look so much like my adopted parents. They are more than good to me. As a matter of fact, they have overly compensated in the area of parenthood, because I am adopted. They have never lied to me, abused me, or neglected me. I have had the best that they had to offer me. Even in the difficult times they have insulated me with their love and care.

I just feel a piece of me is missing. The usual question of why my mother gave me up taunts me and disturbs me. When I am happy, I feel guilty because not knowing my mother makes me sad. Lord, I have tried to reach her, to see myself in her, to get a piece of me from her, and to identify with her. I hope that this is possible, but if not, please give me the grace and peace I need to go on with my life. You said You would be a mother and father to the orphan. I do have parents who love me. I need You to show me how to be satisfied with Your love flowing through them, in order to be at rest in my mind. Thank You, Lord, for being so sensitive to my tender need!

*When my father and my mother forsake me,*
*then the Lord will take me up*
(Psalm 27:10).

*A father of the fatherless, and a judge of the*
*widows, is God in His holy habitation*
(Psalm 68:5).

*For ye have not received the spirit of bondage*
*again to fear; but ye have received the Spirit of*
*adoption, whereby we cry, Abba, Father*
(Romans 8:15).

*To redeem them that were under the law, that we might*
*receive the adoption of sons. And because ye are sons, God*
*hath sent forth the Spirit of His Son into your hearts, crying,*
*Abba, Father. Wherefore thou art no more a servant, but a*
*son; and if a son, then an heir of God through Christ*
(Galatians 4:5-7).

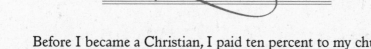
# PRAYER FOR
# TITHING AND GIVING

Before I became a Christian, I paid ten percent to my church and I gave to charity organizations. I had a good job and an increasingly steady income. I know that tithing and giving works, because I have benefited from giving freely and consistently to You, Lord.

I have been saved for a while, and now I have slacked off in my giving. My financial state has been drastically affected because of my diminished giving. I know that You are my source, Lord. I know that Your name is Jehovah Jireh. I know that You make ways out of no way. I have become sloppy and careless.

I want to return to the place of blessing, which is the place of giving. I want to be blessed so that I can be a blessing. Deliver me from the weakness of overspending and release me into prudent expenditure. I will return to tithing and giving, if You help me and minister to my needs. Thank You, Lord!

*Bring ye all the tithes into the storehouse, that
there may be meat in mine house, and prove me now
herewith, saith the Lord of hosts, if I will not open you
the windows of heaven, and pour you out a blessing,
that there shall not be room enough to receive it*
(Malachi 3:10).

*Upon the first day of the week let every one of
you lay by him in store, as God hath prospered
him, that there be no gatherings when I come*
(1 Corinthians 16:2).

*But this I say, He which soweth sparingly shall reap also
sparingly; and he which soweth bountifully shall reap
also bountifully. Every man according as he purposeth
in his heart, so let him give; not grudgingly, or of
necessity: for God loveth a cheerful giver*
(2 Corinthians 9:6-7).

# PRAYER IN THE VALLEY

Today I hear so much about the mountaintop experience of faith that I feel quite guilty talking about the valley. I just don't feel great in the valley. Depression overshadows me, loneliness grabs me, and darkness engulfs me. Why do I have to spend time in the valley? I go to church where everyone seems to be high and lifted up in spirit. What do I do when the praise doesn't come so easily and the Word doesn't touch so quickly?

I am not so childish that I believe You promised me a rose garden. I know there are highs and lows in everyone's life. But teach me how to live in this lowly place. Lord, teach me how to rest in the place of solitude. Lord, let me feel Your arms around me in the stillness of the valley's night. If You teach me how to live in the valley, then I can rise high to the mountaintop. Thank You, Lord!

*Yea, though I walk through the valley of the shadow*
*of death, I will fear no evil: for Thou art with me;*
*Thy rod and Thy staff they comfort me*
(Psalm 23:4).

*Who passing through the valley of Baca make*
*it a well; the rain also filleth the pools*
(Psalm 84:6).

*Every valley shall be exalted, and every mountain*
*and hill shall be made low: and the crooked shall*
*be made straight, and the rough places plain*
(Isaiah 40:4).

# PRAYER DURING MY PENDULUM PERIOD

Swinging back and forth, hanging high and low, and wavering to and fro cause me to be unfocused, unstable, and unwise. Yet, this is where You have me. How do I embrace this or explain this? Is this part of my journey? Am I the only one in the world who feels giddy and unsteady every now and then?

Lord, I know that in this place of uncertainty You have a plan. I am just so consumed with the fluctuation of my life that I can't concentrate on the wisdom of Your Words.

Please calm my spirit, please quiet my fears, and please hold my heart. Teach me the wisdom of unanswered prayers. There is a reason for this temporary upheaval in my life and soul. Help me to find the secret place even in this uneven place. Thank You, Lord!

*God is our refuge and strength, a very present help in trouble.
Therefore will not we fear, though the earth be removed, and
though the mountains be carried into the midst of the sea*
(Psalm 46:1-2).

*Wherein ye greatly rejoice, though now for a season, if
need be, ye are in heaviness through manifold temptations:
that the trial of your faith, being much more precious than
of gold that perisheth, though it be tried with fire, might
be found unto praise and honour and glory at the appearing
of Jesus Christ: whom having not seen, ye love; in whom,
though now ye see Him not, yet believing, ye rejoice
with joy unspeakable and full of glory*
(1 Peter 1:6-8).

*My brethren, count it all joy when ye fall into divers
temptations; knowing this, that the trying of your faith
worketh patience. But let patience have her perfect work,
that ye may be perfect and entire, wanting nothing*
(James 1:2-4).

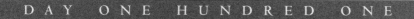

# PRAYER FOR
# A CHALLENGING DAY

The phone rang early this morning and snatched me out of a peaceful sleep. The first call was from a bill collector; then it was a demanding family member; and then there was a knock from a dissatisfied staff member.

Is this really the day that the Lord has made? Will I rejoice and be glad in it before midnight? Lord, I pray that You give me a calm and wise spirit. The agenda of the enemy intends to break my spirit, erode my tranquility, and disarm my faith. Please hold my emotions, cover my sensitive spots, and guide my thoughts and lips.

There are people who have been assigned by the enemy to participate in attempting to demoralize me. Please help me, Lord, to forgive them, but rebuke the spirit and its assignment. Rest, oh my soul, in the Lord! Again, I say, "Rest!"

*Nevertheless God, that comforteth*
*those that are cast down...*
(2 Corinthians 7:6).

*Casting all your care upon Him; for He careth for*
*you....But the God of all grace, who hath called us unto*
*His eternal glory by Christ Jesus, after that ye have suffered*
*a while, make you perfect, stablish, strengthen, settle you*
(1 Peter 5:7,10).

*You will keep in perfect peace him whose*
*mind is steadfast, because he trusts in You*
(Isaiah 26:3 NIV).

# PRAYER AGAINST PRIDE

I thought that proud people were arrogant, rude, and insolent. I did not know that pride meant that I always had to have my way. I didn't realize the subtlety of this insidious spirit. It is the same spirit that caused the devil to be thrown out of Heaven. It is the need to function independent of You, God.

I thought humility was just being nice and showing a good face. It is, however, a matter of the heart. I have shown many good faces, but in my heart I resented—highly—the demands that have been placed on me. I have held it in because I wanted to appear to be a "good" person. In fact, I have been very angry most of the time. The anger has stemmed from being asked to prefer others or think about others differently. I have always, in one way or another, wanted to be first.

This is not your standard of discipleship and servanthood. The irony is that when I prefer others, You, Lord, prefer me. I am so tired of fighting to have my way. When I do have my way, I am still unful-filled. Thank You, Lord, for the desire to change. Please show me my ways that I may commit them unto You for divine intervention and transformation.

*However, Hezekiah humbled the pride of his heart, both he
and the inhabitants of Jerusalem, so that the wrath of the
Lord did not come on them in the days of Hezekiah*
(2 Chronicles 32:26 NAS).

*The fear of the Lord is to hate evil; pride and arrogance
and the evil way, and the perverted mouth, I hate*
(Proverbs 8:13 NAS).

*When pride comes, then comes dishonor,
but with the humble is wisdom*
(Proverbs 11:2 NAS).

# PRAYER TO APPRECIATE MY GIFTS

I have gifts that I have taken for granted, Lord. These gifts may not seem grand or pronounced as a musical gift or an athletic gift, yet I have come to appreciate your gifting in me. The gift to be sensitive is a marvelous endowment. It was dormant for many years, because I was so self-centered. It was through adversity and difficulty that I began to see and hear so much with deeper senses.

I hear joy bells in the midst of sorrow; I feel comforted in the midst of grief; and I feel loved in the midst of rejection. Lord, You have done something so marvelous in me, because in time past, I would be so dull of understanding.

This gift to feel, to hear, to see, and to understand beyond the human plane has given me so much life and hope. I may never become a great singer or orator, but I will live with my eyes wide open and my ears highly sensitized to the inspirational unveiling of Your presence. This is truly a divine gift.

*The law of the Lord is perfect, restoring the soul; the testimony of the Lord is sure, making wise the simple. The precepts of the Lord are right, rejoicing the heart; the commandment of the Lord is pure, enlightening the eyes*
(Psalm 19:7-8 NAS).

*Open my eyes that I may behold wonderful things from Thy law*
(Psalm 119:18 NAS).

*For since the beginning of the world men have not heard, nor perceived by the ear, neither hath the eye seen, O God, beside Thee, what He hath prepared for him that waiteth for Him*
(Isaiah 64:4).

*But as it is written, Eye hath not seen, nor ear heard, neither have entered into the heart of man, the things which God hath prepared for them that love Him*
(1 Corinthians 2:9).

# PRAYER FROM
# ONE WHO IS DOWNSIZED

Well, I don't know where to turn after all these years of working on this job. I thought that this was the job that would set me up for my comfortable retirement. But here I am with a family and short-lived financial package, which is only a tip compared to what I would have gotten, if I had finished my time in my job position.

I have limited skills and the job market is very selective. My spouse needs help with the family's budget and I am extremely aware of the needs of the future. The positive thing is that I was an ardent tithe payer. I gave over and beyond in tithe and offering. The other positive thing is that I kept up with my bills and tried to support my family. However, I did not invest, save, or prepare for this sudden change in my economic condition. *Help!*

I have screamed, cried, and complained. I am now ready to be still and hear what You have to say to me. In my sane moments, I sense that You are calling me to fulfill some of my dreams that I sacrificed for the job. I now see possibilities, but I don't see resources. Teach me how to shift into Your divine guidance and cause me to trust Your providential care for my life. Let's go, God! I am ready for the change. Please help me to keep my trust level up. To God be the glory!

*Ye that fear Jehovah, trust in Jehovah: He is their help and their shield. Jehovah hath been mindful of us; He will bless (us): He will bless the house of Israel; He will bless the house of Aaron. He will bless them that fear Jehovah, both small and great. Jehovah increase you more and more, you and your children*
(Psalm 115:11-14 ASV).

*Bring ye all the tithes into the storehouse, that there may be meat in Mine house, and prove Me now herewith, saith the Lord of hosts, if I will not open you the windows of heaven, and pour you out a blessing, that there shall not be room enough to receive it. And I will rebuke the devourer for your sakes, and he shall not destroy the fruits of your ground; neither shall your vine cast her fruit before the time in the field, saith the Lord of hosts. And all nations shall call you blessed: for ye shall be a delightsome land, saith the Lord of hosts*
(Malachi 3:10-12).

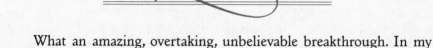
# PRAYER TO
# HANDLE THE MIRACLE

What an amazing, overtaking, unbelievable breakthrough. In my wildest dreams, I never, ever thought that this kind of blessing would come into my life. I am stunned, flabbergasted, and bug-eyed. This blessing is beyond my human and even spiritual expectation.

You are the rewarder of those who diligently seek You. You are able to do more than what we ask or think in our prayers to You. You are true to those who wait for You.

I will not allow this blessing to distract me from my commitment to love, honor, and obey You. Please give me the wisdom to handle this blessing and not abuse Your grace and favor towards me. I will bring structure and order to my life so that I can manage the treasures that You have entrusted in my possession. Thank You, Lord, for the discipline needed to care for Your investment.

*He becometh poor that worketh with a slack hand; but the
hand of the diligent maketh rich*
(Proverbs 10:4 ASV).

*Be diligent in these things; give thyself wholly to them; that
thy progress may be manifest unto all*
(1 Timothy 4:15 ASV).

*But without faith it is impossible to please Him: for he that
cometh to God must believe that He is, and that He is a
rewarder of them that diligently seek Him*
(Hebrews 11:6).

# THE INTERNATIONAL GATHERING AT BETH RAPHA

P.O. Box 684
Pomona, NY 10970

## REV. DR. JACQUELINE E. MCCULLOUGH, SENIOR PASTOR

www.bethrapha.org
www.rizpah.org

# Notes

# Notes

# Notes

# Notes

# Notes

# Notes

# Notes

# Notes